Edwin Arlington Robinson
A Supplementary Bibliography

Edwin Arlington Robinson

A Supplementary Bibliography

By William White
Wayne State University

The Kent State University Press

The Serif Series
Bibliographies and Checklists, Number 17
William White, General Editor
Wayne State University

PS
3535
.O25
Z997

Copyright © 1971 by Kent State University Press
All rights reserved
ISBN 0-87338-107-6
Library of Congress Catalog Card Number 70-126806
Manufactured in the United States of America
At the Press of The Oberlin Printing Company
Designed by Merald E. Wrolstad

First Edition

Contents

Introduction

This bibliography, as the title suggests, is a supplement to Charles
Beecher Hogan's admirable *A Bibliography of Edwin Arlington
Robinson* (New Haven: Yale University Press, 1936), and includes
the material in Mr. Hogan's "Edwin Arlington Robinson: New
Bibliographical Notes," *The Papers of the Bibliographical Society
of America* (New York), Vol. XXXV, pp. 115-144, Second Quarter
1941. Because it is a supplement to the Hogan book, I have followed
his organization and style, with some slight modifications, particularly
in the descriptions of books by Robinson, though I am aware that most
compilations such as this are used by readers more familiar with the
MLA Style Sheet. Although an attempt has been made to be as complete
as possible, and I have listed virtually all of the most readily available
primary and secondary material, I certainly do not approach Mr. Hogan's
work in this respect. While he says (on page iii of his *Bibliography*)
that what he has prepared is "intended primarily for collectors,"
the present supplement is meant for scholars and critics—as well as
librarians and collectors—who would like to know what has been
written on the creator of "Luke Havergal" and "Miniver Cheevy"
during the past thirty-five years. I have also cited earlier material,
omitted from the Hogan *Bibliography*, much of it from Mr. Hogan's
"Notes."

Further, I have included almost all of the items (except the list of
photographs) from Lillian Lippincott's 1937 *Bibliography* which
were missing in my own and the Hogan compilations, more than a
hundred articles, theses, chapters, and reviews.

There are times, which will be obvious from a glance at the

bibliography, when Robinson did not seem to attract the attention
of editors and commentators that a writer of his stature deserves;
such fears, on the other hand, may be dispelled by the 1969 entries
below. This was the hundredth anniversary of his birth, and a year-long
celebration at Colby College included exhibits, performances of his
poems in recitations and song, instruments and impressionistic paintings,
an address by Malcolm Cowley, the four issues of the *Colby Library
Quarterly* devoted exclusively to EAR, and the publication by the
college's press of *Appreciation of Edwin Arlington Robinson:
28 Interpretive Essays*. Other birthday volumes were Professor Ellsworth
Barnard's *Centenary Essays*, the Masterwork Press's *A Tilbury Score*,
and *Edwin Arlington Robinson: A Bio-Bibliography*, issued after
the Trinity College exhibition of the Collamore Collection.

Among the pieces in the *Colby Library Quarterly* was my own
bibliography of Robinson for the years 1964-1969; to this material
I have added a previously published bibliography for 1941-1963,
also in the *CLQ*, considerably revised, all here published in book form
with the kind permission of Professor Richard Cary, editor of the
Colby Library Quarterly. But my principal debt is to Charles Beecher
Hogan, of Woodbridge, Connecticut, who has generously allowed me
to use his material from the *PBSA* in my text and in the appendix,
which consists of Mr. Hogan's own additions and corrections to his
Bibliography of Edwin Arlington Robinson. Mr. Hogan's contribution
has greatly enhanced the usefulness of the present volume.

WILLIAM WHITE

Mashnee Village, Cape Cod
26 February 1971

Part I. Works Separately Published

1937 *Collected Poems*

COLLECTED / POEMS / OF / EDWIN ARLINGTON / ROBINSON / NEW
YORK / THE MACMILLAN COMPANY / 1937 /

Collation: [1]-[ii] + [i]-xii and front. + [1]-1498, as follows:
[i]-[ii] blank; [i] bastard title; [ii] publisher's device and
addresses; front. to face title: reproduction of painting made in
1916 by Lilla Cabot Perry of the author, and beneath, reproduction
of his signature [protected by tissue-paper]; [iii] title-page as
above; [iv] notices of copyrights, reservation of rights, date of
publication, edition, and printing; [v] acknowledgments; [vi]
blank; vii-xii contents; [1]-1488 text; 1489-1492 index to titles;
1493-1498 index to first lines.

Issued in maroon cloth. Stamped in gold on front cover:
reproduction of author's signature. Stamped in gold on spine:
COLLECTED / POEMS / ROBINSON / MACMILLAN / (dot) /. All edges
trimmed. The leaves measure 20.2 by 13.7 cms.

Published April 20, 1937. The original price was $3.00.

Note: Lines 8-14 on page 1312 are a new version of lines 14-20
on page 2 of the first edition of *Amaranth* (1934). See *Edwin Arlington
Robinson*, by H. B. Collamore, 1936, pp. 57-58.

By 1967 there had been seventeen printings of *Collected Poems.*

1940 *Selected Letters*

SELECTED LETTERS / OF / *Edwin Arlington Robinson* / 1940 /
THE MACMILLAN COMPANY / NEW YORK /

Collation: [i]-[ii] + [i]-[xii] and front. + [1]-[194], as follows:

4

[i]-[ii] blank; [i] bastard title; [ii] publisher's device and addresses; front. to face title: reproduction of photograph of author, and beneath, reproduction of his signature; [iii] title-page as above; [iv] notices of copyright, reservation of rights, date of publication, edition, printing, and press-work; [v] quotation from Milton; [vi] blank; vii-x introduction, signed: RIDGELY TORRENCE; [xi] biographical note; [xii] blank; [1]-178 text; [179] sectional half-title: NOTES; [180] blank; 181-191 notes on the text; [192]-[194] blank.

Issued in natural linen cloth. Plate-mark stamped at top of spine, stamped in gold on background of green cloth: SELECTED / LETTERS / OF / EDWIN / ARLINGTON / ROBINSON / (The whole inclosed within a heavy rule within a light rule). Stamped in green at bottom of spine: MACMILLAN / (dot) /. All edges trimmed. The leaves measure 21.3 by 14.3 cms.

Published February 20, 1940. The original price was $2.50.

Note: The book contains no index of the recipients of the letters. This index is as follows:

1943 *Letters to Howard George Schmitt*

LETTERS / OF / Edwin Arlington Robinson (in red) / TO /Howard George Schmitt / (flower in red) / *Edited by Carl J. Weber* / *WATERVILLE, MAINE* / COLBY COLLEGE LIBRARY / 1943 /

Collation: [i]-[viii] + [1]-[40], as follows: [i]-[iv] blank; [v] bastard title; [vi] blank; [vii] title-page as above; [viii] notice of copyright; [1] half-title; [2] blank; 3-31 text; [32] blank; [33] notices of permission, press-work, limitation of edition, with editor's autograph number [34]-[40] blank.

Issued in decorated paper in purple, pink and black on boards, with white backstrip. Printed in black on spine, reading upwards: *LETTERS OF EDWIN ARLINGTON ROBINSON TO HOWARD GEORGE SCHMITT /*. Fore and bottom edges untrimmed; top edge trimmed. The leaves measure 24 by 15.2 cms.

Published July 15, 1943, in an edition of 200 numbered copies. The original price was $2.50.

Contains: Sixty-six letters to Howard G. Schmitt, dated between *January 9, 1929* and *January 22, 1935*, with the editor's commentary and notes. (Not printed elsewhere.)

1947 *Untriangulated Stars*

Untriangulated (in heavy script) / Stars (in heavy script, with six irregular stars around title) /LETTERS OF / EDWIN ARLINGTON ROBINSON / TO HARRY DE FOREST SMITH / 1890-1905 / EDITED BY DENHAM SUTCLIFFE / • HARVARD UNIVERSITY PRESS — CAMBRIDGE — *1947* • /

Collation: [i]-[xxviii] + [1]-348, as follows:[1] quotation; [ii] notice of British publisher; [iii] title-page as above; [iv] notices of copyright and printing; [v] dedication; [vi] blank; [vii] contents [viii] blank; ix-xi preface (signed: DENHAM SUTCLIFFE *Kenyon College Gambier, Ohio March,* 1947); [xii] blank; xiii-xxvii introduction; [xxviii] blank; [1] half-title to Part I; [2] blank; 3-25 text; [26] blank; [27] half-title to Part II; [28] blank; 29-103 text [104] blank; [105] half-title to Part III; [106] blank; 107-290 text; [291] half-title to Part IV; [292] blank; 293-308 text; [309] half-title to notes; [310] blank; 311-327 notes; [328] blank; [329] half-title to index; [330] blank; 331-348 index.

Issued in red cloth. Stamped in gold on purple design on front cover: Untriangulated (in heavy script) / Stars (in heavy script, with six irregular stars around title) /. Stamped in purple on spine: (star in gold) / EDITED BY / DENHAM / SUTCLIFFE / UNTRIANGULATED STARS (in gold on purple design, reading downwards) / HARVARD / UNIVERSITY / PRESS / (rule in gold) /. All edges trimmed. The leaves measure 22.2 by 15 cms.

Published November 6, 1947, in an edition of 4,000 copies. The original price was $5.00.

Contains: One hundred and sixty-one letters to Harry de Forest Smith, dated between *September 27, 1890* and *August 30, 1905,* of the 191 in the Houghton Library at Harvard. (Thirty letters are reprinted in *Selected Early Poems and Letters,* 1960.)

1948 *Vachel Lindsay*

V (in blue) ACHEL LINDSAY / by / Edwin Arlington Robinson / (decoration in blue) / Privately Printed for John S. Mayfield / By the Fraternity Press / Washington, D. C. / 1948 /

Collation: [1]-[4], as follows: [1] title-page as above; [2] facsimile of letter; [3] text; [4] note, notices of limitation of edition, with editor's autograph number.

Issued in paper covers, stapled. Printed in black on front cover: VACHEL LINDSAY / by Edwin Arlington Robinson / (decoration) /. All edges trimmed. The leaves measure 27.8 by 21.4 cms.

Not formally published. Issued in an edition of 100 numbered copies. The edition was prepared not for sale, but for private distribution.

Contains: Letter to John S. Mayfield, dated: *January 6, 1932.* (Reproduced, in both facsimile and type, in *The Courier* [Syracuse University], Vol. III, pp. 28, 29, June 1963.)

1953 *Tilbury Town*

TILBURY TOWN / *SELECTED POEMS OF* / EDWIN ARLINGTON
ROBINSON / *Introduction and Notes* / by LAWRANCE THOMPSON /
THE MACMILLAN COMPANY / NEW YORK 1933 / (Title-page
printed in black on blue with white border)

Collation: [i]-xvi + [1]-144, as follows: [i] bastard title, [ii]
quotation in black on blue with white border; [iii] title-page as
above; [iv] notices of copyright, reservation of rights, printing,
and press-work; v-vii contents; [viii] blank; ix-xvi introduction;
[1] half-title to Part I, "Predicaments"; [2] blank; 3-42 text; [43]
half-title to Part II, "Passions"; [44] blank; 45-70 text; [71]
half-title to Part III, "The Dead"; [72] blank; 73-96 text;
[97] half-title to Part IV; "Edge of Town"; [98] blank; 99-120
text; [121] half-title to Part V, "Against the Sky"; [122]
blank; 123-131 text; [132] blank; 133-143 notes; 144 index.

Issued in blue cloth with black backstrip. Stamped in silver on front
cover: TILBURY TOWN/ *Selected Poems of /Edwin Arlington Robinson /.*
Stamped in silver on spine, reading downwards: TILBURY TOWN •
Selected Poems of Edwin Arlington Robinson • MACMILLAN /. All edges
trimmed. The leaves measure 22.3 by 15.2 cms.

Published October 6, 1953. The original price was $3.50.

Contains: Sixty-five poems (reprinted); excerpts of letters to George
W. Latham, *1893,* p. xv; to Arthur R. Gledhill, *December 26, 1894,*
p. 135; to Edith Brower, *March 15, 1914,* p. 137; to Carl J. Weber,
January 28, 1923, p. 139; and to an admirer, *January 7, 1932,* p. 143.
(Not printed elsewhere, except for excerpt to Edith Brower in
Letters to Edith Brower [see below], p. 155.)

1960 *Selected Early Poems and Letters*

(Three decorations) / Edwin Arlington Robinson / *Selected Early Poems* / *and Letters* / EDITED BY CHARLES T. DAVIS / *Princeton University* / *Holt, Rinehart and Winston* / NEW YORK /

Collation: [i]-[xxxii] + [1]-[240], as follows: [i] title-page as above; [ii] notices of permission, copyrights, Library of Congress catalogue card number, and printing; [iii] dedication; [iv] blank; v-viii contents; [ix]-xxiii introduction; [xxiv]-xxvi chronology; [xxvii]-xxx bibliography; [xxxi] textual note; [xxxii] blank; [1] half-title to "Early Poems"; [2] blank; [3]-180 text; [181] half-title to "Letters"; [182] blank; [183]-222 text; [223]-238 notes; [239]-[240] list of Rinehart Editions.

Issued in salmon colored paperback. Printed in black on front cover: $1.45 / *Rinehart Editions* / (rule in white) / EDWIN ARLINGTON ROBINSON / SELECTED EARLY / POEMS AND LETTERS / EDITED BY CHARLES T. DAVIS / HOLT, RINEHART AND WINSTON, INC. (in white) / (rule) / 107 / *RE* (in white) /. Printed in black on spine, reading downwards: ROBINSON • *Selected Early Poems and Letters* / 107 / *RE* /. All edges trimmed. The leaves measure 18.2 by 12.4 cms.

Published November 21, 1960. The original price was $1.45. Reprinted with variant paperback covers.

Contains: Sixty poems reprinted from *The Torrent and The Night Before* and *The Children of the Night: A Book of Poems*, and 16 from *Captain Craig: A Book of Poems*; 30 letters to Harry de Forest Smith from *Untriangulated Stars*, 3 to Daniel Gregory Mason and 1 to Josephine Preston Peabody from *Selected Letters*.

1965 *Selected Poems*

SELECTED / POEMS / of / *Edwin Arlington* / *Robinson* / (rule / EDITED BY / MORTON DAUWEN ZABEL / With an introduction by James Dickey / (rule) / THE MACMILLAN COMPANY, NEW YORK / Collier-Macmillan Limited, London /

Collation: [i]-[xxx] + [1]-[258], as follows: [i] bastard title; [ii] blank; [iii] title-page as above; [iv] notices of copyright, reservation of rights, Library of Congress catalogue card number, and printing; v-ix contents; [x] blank; xi-xxviii introduction (signed: JAMES DICKEY *March, 1965*), [xxix] half-title; [xxx] blank; [1] half-title to "The Children of the Night" and dedication; [2] blank; 3-19 text; [20] blank; [21] half-title to "Captain Craig" and dedication; [22] blank; 23-61 text; [62] blank; [63] half-title to "The Town Down the River" and dedication; [64] blank; 65-98 text; [99] half-title to "The Man Against the Sky" and dedication; [100] blank; 101-156 text; [157] half-title to "The Three Taverns" and dedication; [158] blank; 159-189 text; [190] blank; [191] half-title to "Avon's Harvest" and dedication; [192] blank; 193-206 text; [207] half-title to "Dionysus in Doubt" and dedication; [208] blank; 209-223 text; [224] blank; [225] half-title to "Nicodemus" and dedication; [226] blank; 227-244; [245] half-title to editor's note, bibliography, and index; [246] blank; 247-254 editor's note and bibliography; 255-257 index of titles; [258] blank.

Issued in blue-green cloth. Stamped in gold on spine: ZABEL / (decorated rule) / *Selected / Poems / of / Edwin /Arlington / Robinson* / (decorated rule) / MACMILLAN /. All edges trimmed. Top edge colored red. The leaves measure 21 by 14 cms.

Published September 13, 1965. The original price was $5.00, the paperback price $1.95. Reprinted in paperback as a Collier Books edition, 1966, second printing 1968, third 1969, fourth 1970.

Contains: One hundred and nineteen poems reprinted from various Robinson books (see *Collation* above).

Note: James Dickey's introduction, "Edwin Arlington Robinson: The Many Truths," was reprinted in *Edwin Arlington Robinson: A Collection of Critical Essays* (Englewood Cliffs, New Jersey: Prentice-Hall, Inc., 1970), pp. 77-94.

1968 *Letters to Edith Brower*

Edwin Arlington Robinson's / LETTERS TO / Edith Brower / edited by / RICHARD CARY / The Belknap Press of Harvard University Press / CAMBRIDGE • MASSACHUSETTS • 1968 /

Collation: [i]-[xii] + 1-[236], as follows: [i] bastard title; [ii] blank;

[iii] title-page as above; [iv] notices of copyright, reservation of rights, distribution, Library of Congress catalogue card number, and printing; [v] dedication; [vi] blank; vii acknowledgments; [viii] blank; ix contents; [x] blank; [xi] half-title; [xii] photographs of Edwin Arlington Robinson and Edith Brower; 1-12 introduction; [13] half-title; [14] blank; 15-199 text; [200] blank; [201] half-title to appendixes and index; [202] blank; 203-215 Appendix I, *Memories of Edwin Arlington Robinson*, by Edith Brower; 216-224 Appendix II, *Edwin Arlington Robinson*, by Edith Brower; 225-226 Appendix III, *Books by Edwin Arlington Robinson*; 227-233 index; [234]-[236] blank.

Issued in pale tan cloth, with light tan backstrip. Stamped in black on spine: *Cary* / (rule) /*Edwin* / *Arlington* / *Robinson's* / *Letters* / *to* / *Edith* / *Brower* / (rule) / *Belknap* / *Harvard* /. All edges trimmed. The leaves measure 23.4 by 15 cms.

Published July 1, 1968, in an edition of 2,000 copies. The original price was $7.95.

Contains: One hundred and eighty-nine letters to Edith Brower, dated between *January 13, 1897* and *June 1, 1930*, with the editor's commentary and notes. (Not printed elsewhere, except for excerpts in *Tilbury Town* [1953], *Maine Summer* [1939], *Colby Library Quarterly*, Series I, p. 30, March 1943; Series VI, pp. 181-183, December 1962; Series VI, pp. 235-244, June 1963; *Victorian Newsletter*, No. 23, pp. 19-21; and *American Notes & Queries*, Vol. II, pp. 35-36, November 1963).

1969 *A Tilbury Score*

A / TILBURY / SCORE / "What shall we do with Robinson?" / Theodore Roosevelt / (design) / *MASTERWORKS PRESS* / *BASSETT FOUNDATION* / SUMMIT, N. J. /

Collation: Seventeen unnumbered leaves (i.e., [i]-[iv] + [1]-[30]), as follows: [i]-[iii] blank, folded over; [iv] front. to face title: reproduction of drawing of E. A. Robinson; [1] title-page as above; [2] notices of acknowledgment and copyright; [3] introduction, "A Centennial Occasion" (signed Peter Darien *May 31, 1969*); [4] blank; [5]-[26] text; [27]-[28] blank; [29]

notices of limitation of edition, with number in black ink, design, paper, cover, and typeface; [30] blank.

Issued in heavy gray paper wrappers, sewn, the cover folded over. Printed in black on front cover: A TILBURY SCORE / (reproduction of author's signature) /. All edges trimmed. The leaves measure 17.8 by 12.4 cms.

Published November 14, 1969, in an edition of 500 numbered copies "to honor his [Robinson's] centennial." The original price was $4.00

Contains: Twenty-two sonnets from *Sonnets 1889-1927*.

Part II. Work Originally Published in Books and Pamphlets

1904 *Our Phonographic Poets*

Our / Phonographic Poets / (triple rule) / (ornament representing an open book) / WRITTEN BY STENOGRAPHERS / & TYPISTS UPON SUBJECTS / PERTAINING TO THEIR ARTS / *Compiled by* / *"TOPSY TYPIST"* / (rule) / PRICE 25 CENTS / (rule) / 1904 / (rule) / NEW YORK / POPULAR PUBLISHING COMPANY / 337 BROADWAY /

Collation: [1]-[136], as follows: [1] title-page as above; [2] notice of copyright; [3] dedication; [4] blank; [5]-126 text; [127] notice of advertisements to follow; 128-135 advertisements; [136] blank.

Issued in natural light tan paper wrapper. Printed in dark brown on front cover: OUR / PHONOGRAPHIC / POETS / (The initial "P" of "PHONOGRAPHIC" extending from the top to the bottom of the three lines) (The whole inclosed within a dark brown rule). All edges trimmed and colored red, both fore corners rounded. The leaves measure 13 by 8.4 cms.

Published July 13, 1904. From contemporary advertisements and from an advertisement in the book itself (page 131), it would appear that it was issued not only in paper at 25 cents, but also in Russia leather at 50 cents and in Morocco and gilt at $1.00. "Topsy Typist" is a pseudonym for Enoch Newton Miner.

Contains: *Isaac Pitman*, pp. 79-80. (Originally published in *The Phonographic World*, Vol. V, p. 280, May 1890. See *The*

14

Colophon, N. S., Vol. III, pp. 359-363, Summer 1938. See Part V, below.)

1914   *The Edward MacDowell Association Report for 1913*

THE EDWARD MACDOWELL / MEMORIAL ASSOCIATION / REPORT / FOR
.THE YEAR 1913 / NEW YORK / THE IRVING PRESS / 1914 /

Collation: front. + [1]-[28], as follows: front. to face title:
reproduction of photograph of "Hillcrest"; [1] title-page as above;
[2] blank; [3] list of officers of The Edward MacDowell
Memorial Association; [4] blank; 5-27 text; [28] blank.

Issued in natural tan paper wrapper. Printed in dark brown on
front cover: THE / EDWARD MACDOWELL / MEMORIAL ASSOCIATION /
REPORT / FOR THE YEAR 1913 /. All edges untrimmed. The leaves
measure 23 by 15.5 cms. Three full-page illustrations in the text
on glossy paper.

Not formally published. Issued *ca.* April 1914. The edition was
prepared not for sale, but for private distribution.

Contains: Letter to Caroline B. Dow, dated: *26 March, 1913*,
p. 9. (Not printed elsewhere.)

1927   *Roosevelt as We Knew Him*

ROOSEVELT / AS WE KNEW HIM / THE PERSONAL RECOLLECTIONS / OF
ONE HUNDRED AND FIFTY OF / HIS FRIENDS AND ASSOCIATES /
By / FREDERICK S. WOOD / WITH A PREFATORY NOTE BY / CALVIN
COOLIDGE / (device) / THE JOHN C. WINSTON COMPANY /
PHILADELPHIA AND CHICAGO /

Collation: [i]-[xxii] and front. + 1-[490], as follows: [i] bastard title;
[ii] blank; front. to face title: reproduction of photograph of
Theodore Roosevelt, and beneath, reproduction of his signature;
[iii] title-page as above; [iv] notices of copyright, publisher's
device, printing, press-work, and the word "Roosevelt"; [v]
dedication; [vi] blank; vii-viii prefatory note; ix-xi preface [xii]
blank; xiii-xvi contents; xvii list of illustrations; [xviii] blank,
xix-xxi introduction; [xxii] blank; 1-481 text; [482] blank;
483-488 index; [489]-[490] blank.

Issued in dark green cloth. Stamped in gold on front cover:
ROOSEVELT / AS WE KNEW HIM / FREDERICK S. WOOD /, inclosed within
light rule within heavy rule stamped in blind around edges. Stamped
in gold on spine: (heavy rule in blind) / (light rule in blind) /
ROOSEVELT / AS WE / KNEW HIM / (rule) / WOOD / WINSTON / (light
rule in blind) / (heavy rule in blind) /. Top edge gilt; fore and bottom
edges trimmed. The leaves measure 21.7 cm. by 14.7 cm. Seven full-
page illustrations in the text on glossy paper.

Published February 1, 1927 in an edition of 1,000 copies. The
original price was $3.50.

Contains: Tribute to Theodore Roosevelt, pp. 391-393. (Not
printed elsewhere. See Part V.)

1928 *A Tribute to Professor Morris Raphael Cohen*

A TRIBUTE / TO PROFESSOR / MORRIS RAPHAEL COHEN / TEACHER &
PHILOSOPHER (in red) / PUBLISHED BY / "THE YOUTH WHO SAT
AT HIS FEET" / NEW YORK MCMXXVIII / (The whole inclosed
within a rule in red)

Collation: [i]-xix + [2]-[110] and front., as follows: [i] bastard
title; [ii] blank; front. to face title: reproduction of portrait of
Professor Cohen; [iii] title-page as above; [iv] acknowledgment of
the painter of the portrait: Joseph Margulies, notices of copyright
and printing; v-vi contents; vii-xii bibliography of published
writings of Professor Cohen; xiii-xix introduction and dedication
(signed; Max Grossman): [2]-106 text; 107-108 list of committee;
109 acknowledgment to the committee; [110] blank.

Issued in purple cloth. Stamped in gold on front cover:
reproduction of Professor Cohen's signature, inclosed within a rule
stamped in blind around edges. Stamped in gold on spine, reading
downwards: MORRIS RAPHAEL COHEN /. All edges trimmed. The
leaves measure 18.8 by 12.7 cms.

Not formally published. Issued 1928 not for sale, but for private
distribution.

Contains: Letter to Max Grossman, dated: *September 18, 1927,*
p. 85. (Not printed elsewhere.)

1929 *Letters of Salutation and Felicitation*

LETTERS *of* SALUTATION / *and* FELICITATION / RECEIVED BY / WILLIAM GILLETTE / ON THE OCCASION OF / *His* FAREWELL TO THE STAGE *in* / "SHERLOCK HOLMES" /

Collation: Sixty-three unnumbered leaves (i. e., [1]-[126]), as follows: [1] Alphabetical Order of the Letters, with addendum slip attached; [2] blank; [3]-[125] text; [126] blank. The letters are printed on the recto of each leaf only, and each leaf has a line of perforation approximately 2 cms. from the top.

Issued in light blue paper wrappers, the title printed on the front cover, and bound along the top edge. All edges trimmed. The leaves measure 15 by 10.2 cms.

Not formally published. Issued November 25, 1929 not for sale, but for private distribution.

Contains: Letter to William Gillette, dated: *30 Ipswich Street, Boston, October 17, 1929,* p. [100]. (Not printed elsewhere.)

1932 *Our Times: The United States, 1900-1925*

OUR TIMES / THE UNITED STATES / 1900-1925 / IV / THE WAR BEGINS / 1909-1914/ BY / MARK SULLIVAN / CHARLES SCRIBNER'S SONS / NEW YORK (dot) LONDON / 1932 /

Collation: [i]-[xxii] + 1-[632], as follows: [i] bastard title; [ii] blank; [iii] title-page as above; [iv] notices of copyright, printing, reservation of rights, and printer's imprint; v-x table of contents; xi-xx list of illustrations; [xxi] half-title; [xxii] blank; 1-612 text; [613] half-title to index; [614] blank; 615-629 index; [630]-[632] blank.

Issued in dark blue cloth. Stamped in blind on front cover: circle containing an ornament representing an hour-glass with large wings on either side of it, surrounded by: (dot) OUR TIMES (dot) THE UNITED STATES (dot), and at the bottom of the circle: 1900-1925. Stamped in gold on spine: (rule) / OUR / TIMES / (four stars) / THE WAR / BEGINS / 1909-1914 / MARK / SULLIVAN / SCRIBNERS / (rule) /. Top edge trimmed; fore edge untrimmed; bottom edge rough-trimmed. The leaves measure 22.6 by 15.3 cms.

Published 1932. The original price was $3.75.

Contains: Letter to Mark Sullivan, dated: *1926*, p. 107. (Not printed elsewhere.)

1936 *Movers and Shakers*

MABEL DODGE LUHAN / *Movers and Shakers* / VOLUME THREE OF / INTIMATE MEMORIES / (device) / HARCOURT, BRACE AND COMPANY / NEW YORK / (The whole inclosed within an ornamental rule)

Collation: [i]-[viii] and front. + [1]-[544], as follows: [1] bastard title; [ii] list of author's works; front. to face title: reproduction of photograph of author; [iii] title-page as above; [iv] notices of copyright, reservation of rights, edition, printing, press-work, and typography; v-vi contents; [vii] list of illustrations; [viii] blank; [1]-535 text; [536] blank; 537-542 index; [543]-[544] blank.

Issued in dark blue cloth. Stamped in blind on front cover: (ornamental rule) / *Intimate Memories* / MABEL DODGE LUHAN / (ornamental rule) /. Stamped in gold on spine: (ornamental rule in blind) / *Movers* / *and Shakers* / MABEL DODGE / LUHAN / (ornamental rule in blind) / HARCOURT, BRACE / AND COMPANY /. Top edge colored orange; fore edge untrimmed; bottom edge trimmed. The leaves measure 23.4 by 16 cms. Fifteen full-page illustrations in the text on glossy paper.

Published November 19, 1936 in an edition of 3,600 copies. The original price was $5.00.

Contains: Six letters to the author, pp. 136-139. (Not printed elsewhere.)

Note: Mrs. Luhan's LORENZO IN TAOS, New York: Alfred A. Knopf, 1932, contains on the inside front flap of the dust wrapper an excerpt from a letter to the author, not printed elsewhere.

1938 *The Colophon—New Series, Volume III, Number I*

THE / COLOPHON / *new series* / A QUARTERLY FOR BOOKMEN /
(design in orange representing a man lifting a rock) / (rule in
orange) / WINTER 1938 / VOLUME III (dot) NEW SERIES (dot)
NUMBER I / NEW YORK /

Collation: [i]-[vi] + [1]-[170], as follows: [i]-[vi] blank; [1]
title-page as above; [2] notices of publication, subscription,
publisher's address, date of establishment, edition, copyright, date
of publication, and list of editors and contributing editors; [3]
half-title to contents; [4]-[6] contents; 7-142 text; [143] notice of
advertisements, etc. to follow; [144] blank; 145-164 advertisements, "The Crow's Nest," and notes about contributors; 164
colophon; [165]-[170] blank.

Issued in light gray linen cloth. Stamped in rust on front cover:
The / (rule) / COLOPHON / (rule) / (design representing a woman
bathing in a well and four men reading) / (rule) / A QUARTERLY /
FOR BOOKMEN / (rule) / Winter 1938 / (The above inclosed by
double vertical rules) (The whole inclosed within a rule within
an ornamental rule). Stamped in rust on spine: (ornamental rule) /
NEW / SERIES / (plate-mark, stamped in light gray: (dot) The
COLOPHON (dot)) / WINTER / 1938/ (rule) / Volume / III
/ Number / 1/ (ornamental rule) / (The lettering of the above,
from "NEW" *to* "1938" reads downwards). All edges trimmed. The
leaves measure 23.4 by 15.1 cms.

Published March 7, 1938 in an edition of 3,000 copies. The
original price was $10.00 for the year, and $2.80 for individual copies.

Contains: *For Harriet Moody's Cook Book*, p. [92], and
reproduced in facsimile, p. [95]. (Not printed elsewhere. See Part V.)

1938 *A Poet's Life*

A / POET'S LIFE / *Seventy Years* / *in a Changing World* / by HARRIET
MONROE / (ornament) / NEW YORK / THE MACMILLAN
COMPANY / 1938 / (The whole inclosed within a heavy rule
within a double light rule)

Collation: [i]-[ii] + [i]-[xii] and front. + 1-[490], as follows:

[i]-[ii] blank; [i] bastard title; [ii] publisher's device and
addresses; front to face title: reproduction of photograph of author;
[iii] title-page as above; [iv] notices of copyright, printing,
reservation of rights, date of publication, and edition; [v]
acknowledgments; [vi] blank; vii-viii contents; [ix] list of
illustrations; [x] blank; [xi] half-title; [xii] blank; 1-476 text;
477-488 index; [489]-[490] blank.

Issued in light green cloth. Stamped in dark green on front cover:
A / POET'S LIFE / (star) / HARRIET /MONROE /. Stamped in dark green
on spine: (rule in blind) / (ornamental rule) / (rule in blind) / (rule
in blind) / (ornamental rule) / (rule in blind) / (plate-mark, stamped:
A / POET'S / LIFE / (star) / HARRIET / MONROE /) / (rule
in blind) / (ornamental rule) / (rule in blind) / (rule in blind) /
(ornamental rule) / (rule in blind) / (rule in blind) / (ornamental
rule) / (rule in blind) / (rule in blind) / (rule in blind) / (ornamental
rule) / (rule in blind) / MACMILLAN / (rule in blind) / (ornamental
rule) / (rule in blind) /. All edges trimmed. The leaves measure
23.4 by 15.5 cms. Twenty-nine full-page illustrations in the text
on sixteen leaves of glossy paper.

Published March 8, 1938. The original price was $5.00.

Contains: Letter to the author, dated: *January 14, 1913*, p. 254, and
reproduced in facsimile between pp. 254-255. (Published, in large
part, in *Poetry*, Vol. XLVII, p. 34, October 1935, and in *Modern
Philology*, Vol. LX, p. 32, August 1962.)

1938 *Edwin Arlington Robinson*

EDWIN ARLINGTON / ROBINSON / A BIOGRAPHY / BY / HERMANN
  HAGEDORN / NEW YORK / THE MACMILLAN COMPANY / 1938 /
  (The whole inclosed within a double rule within a single rule)

Collation: [i]-[xiv] and front. + 1-402, as follows: [i] bastard title;
  [ii] publisher's device and address; front, to face title: reproduction
  of photograph of Edwin Arlington Robinson, and beneath,
  reproduction of his signature; [iii] title-page as above; [iv]
  notices of copyright, reservation of rights, date of publication,
  printing, and press-work; [v] dedication; [vi] blank; [vii]

quotation from Edwin Arlington Robinson; [viii] blank; ix-x foreword; xi-xii contents; [xiii] half-title; [xiv] blank; 1-384 text; 385-392 list of authorities; 393-402 index.

Issued in cinnamon brown cloth. Plate-mark stamped on front cover, stamped in gold on background of black cloth: EDWIN ARLINGTON / ROBINSON / (The whole inclosed within a light rule within a heavy rule). Plate-mark stamped at top of spine, stamped in gold on background of black cloth: (heavy rule) / (light rule) / EDWIN / ARLINGTON / ROBINSON / (rule) / HAGEDORN / (light rule) / (heavy rule) /. Stamped in gold at bottom of spine: MACMILLAN / (square) (dash) (square) /. All edges trimmed. The leaves measure 21.1 by 14.1 cms.

Published October 4, 1938. The original price was $3.00.

Contains: Remarks, letters, and excerpts from letters, *passim*. (For the most part, not printed elsewhere.)

1938 *Music in My Time*

DANIEL GREGORY MASON / MUSIC / IN MY TIME / AND OTHER REMINISCENCES / THE MACMILLAN COMPANY (dot) NEW YORK (dot) 1938 /

Collation: [i]-[xiv] and front. + 1-[401], as follows: [i] bastard title; [ii] publisher's device and addresses; front. to face title: reproduction of photograph of several well-known musicians, taken in 1913; [iii] title-page as above; [iv] notices of copyright, reservation of rights, date of publication, printing, and press-work; [v] dedication; [vi] quotations from Josiah Royce, William Ernest Hocking, and William Vaughn Moody; [vii] poem by Mr. Mason; [viii] acknowledgments; [ix] contents; [x] blank; [xi]-[xii] list of illustrations; [xiii] half-title; [xiv] blank; 1-402 text; 403-409 index; [410] blank.

Issued in dark blue cloth. Stamped in gold on front cover: design representing musical instruments and wreaths. Stamped in gold on spine: DANIEL / GREGORY / MASON / MUSIC / IN / MY TIME / AND OTHER / REMINISCENCES / MACMILLAN / (dash) (square) (dash) /. All edges trimmed. The leaves measure 23.3 by 15.4 cms. Thirty-five full-page (thirty-one on glossy paper) and six part-page illustrations in the text.

Published November 9, 1938. The original price was $5.00.

Contains: I — Excerpts from twenty-three letters to the author, pp. 83-89, 116-118, 121-129, 133-134. (Originally published in *The Virginia Quarterly Review*, Vol. XIII, pp. 54-56, 58-64, 66-69, Winter 1937, and pp. 225, 227-229, 238-239, Spring 1937, and in *The Yale Review*, Vol. XXV, p. 862, June 1936.)

II — Excerpt from letter to Mrs. Mason, p. 124. (Not printed elsewhere.)

III — Letter to the author, pp. 129-132, and partially reproduced in facsimile, p. 131. (Originally published in *The Virginia Quarterly Review*, Vol. XIII, pp. 231-233, Spring, 1937.)

1938 *Poets at Prayer*

POETS / AT PRAYER / *by* / Sister Mary James Power, S.S.N.D. / (rule) / SHEED & WARD / NEW YORK *and* LONDON / 1938 /

Collation: [i]-[ii] + [i]-xxxvi + [1]-[218], as follows: [i]-[ii] blank; [i] bastard title; [ii] blank; [iii] title-page as above; [iv] notices of copyright, printing, press-work, and date of publication; [v] notice of imprimatur; [vi] blank; [vii] dedication; [viii] blank; ix-x table of contents; xi-xiv acknowledgments; xv-xxi preface; [xxii] blank; xxiii-xxvi foreword; [xxvii] half-title to introduction; [xxviii] blank; xxix-xxxvi introduction; [1]-204 text; 205-214 notes; [215]-[218] blank.

Issued in brown cloth. Stamped in silver on spine: SISTER / MARY / JAMES / POWER / POETS AT PRAYER (these three words reading downwards) / SHEED / & / WARD /. Top edge colored red. Fore and bottom edges untrimmed. The leaves measure 21.5 by 14 cms.

Published December 5, 1938. The original price was $3.00.

Contains: Letter to the author, dated: *January 21, 1930*, p. [72], and reproduced in facsimile on opposite leaf. (Not printed elsewhere.)

1939 *Autobiography with Letters*

WILLIAM LYON PHELPS / (ornament) / AUTOBIOGRAPHY / WITH LETTERS / (ornament) / OXFORD UNIVERSITY PRESS / NEW YORK LONDON TORONTO / 1939 /

Collation: [i]-[ii] + [i]-[xxiv] and front. + [1]-[990], as follows:

[i]-[ii] blank; [i] bastard title; [ii] blank; front. to face title: reproduction of photograph of author; [iii] title-page as above; [iv] notices of copyright, and printing; [v] dedication; [vi] acknowledgment; [vii]-ix preface; [x] blank; [xi]-xvi contents; [xvii]-xxiii introduction; [xxiv] blank; [1] half-title; [2] blank; [3]-972 text; [973]-986 index; [987]-[990] blank.

Issued in bright blue cloth. Stamped in gold on spine: (double rule) / PHELPS / (double rule) / *Auto-* / *biography* / *With* / *Letters* / (double rule) / OXFORD / (double rule) /. Top edge colored blue; fore and bottom edges trimmed. The leaves measure 21.4 by 13.2 cms. Thirty-two full page illustrations in the text (thirty-one on sixteen leaves of glossy paper).

Published April 13, 1939 in edition of 10,000 copies. The original price was $3.75.

Contains: Two letters to the author, dated: *November 18, 1929* and *November 20, 1929*, pp. 696-697. (Originally published in *New York Herald Tribune*, November 13, 1936, pp. 14-15.)

1939 *Maine Summer*

MAINE / SUMMER / (design representing a belfry) / *By* EDWIN VALENTINE MITCHELL / *Illustrated by* / RUTH LEPPER / COWARD-MCCANN, INC. / NEW YORK /

Collation: [1]-[212], as follows: [1] bastard title, [2] list of author's works; [3] title-page as above; [4] notices of copyright, reservation of rights, printing, and press-work; [5] dedication; [6] blank; [7] acknowledgments; [8] blank; [9] contents; [10] blank; [11] half-title; [12] blank; 13-202 text; 203-210 index; [211]-[212] blank.

Issued in light reddish-brown cloth. Stamped in gold on spine: (rule) / (ornamental rule) / (rule) / (ornamental rule) / (rule) / (ornamental rule) / (rule) / (ornamental rule) / (rule) / (plate-mark, stamped in gold on background of bright blue cloth: MAINE /SUMMER / EDWIN / VALENTINE / MITCHELL /) / (rule) / (ornamental rule) / (rule) / (ornamental rule) / (rule) / (ornamental rule) / (rule) / (ornamental rule) / (rule) / COWARD / MCCANN /. Top edge colored blue; fore edge untrimmed; bottom edge rough-trimmed. The leaves measure 21.5 by 14.7 cms. Sixty part-page illustrations in the text. Decorated end-papers.

Published June 23, 1939. The original price was $2.50.

Contains: I — Excerpts from two letters to Edith Brower, dated: *February 1897*, pp. 64-65 (Published in full in *Letters to Edith Brower*, 1968.)

II — Excerpt from undated letter "to a relative" [*i.e.*, Mrs. William Nivison], p. 65. (Not printed elsewhere.)

1940 *Philosophy in the Poetry of Edwin Arlington Robinson*

PHILOSOPHY / IN THE POETRY OF / Edwin Arlington Robinson / ESTELLE KAPLAN / (ornament) / NEW YORK: MORNINGSIDE HEIGHTS / COLUMBIA UNIVERSITY PRESS / 1940 /

Collation: [i]-[xii] + [1]-[164], as follows: [i] bastard title; [ii] blank; [iii] title-page as above; [iv] notices of copyright, foreign agents of the publisher, and printing; [v] dedication; [vi] blank; [vii] note concerning the Columbia Studies in American Culture, and list of Board of Editors; [viii] blank; [ix] acknowledgments; [x] blank; [xi]contents; [xii] blank; [1]-144 text; 145-153 bibliography; [154] blank; 155-162 index; [163]-[164] blank.

Issued in dark blue cloth. Stamped in blind on front cover: device of Columbia University Press, inclosed in rule stamped around edges. Black leather label at top of spine, stamped in gold: (triple rule) / Philosophy / in the / Poetry / of / Edwin / Arlington / Robinson / (ornament) / KAPLAN / (triple rule) /. Stamped in gold in middle of spine: (star) COLUMBIA STUDIES (star) AMERICAN CULTURE (set in the form of a circle) / IN (surrounded by four stars) /. Stamped in gold at bottom of spine: COLUMBIA /. Top edge spattered with dark blue. Fore and bottom edges trimmed. The leaves measure 22.9 by 15 cms.

Published May 20, 1940 in an edition of 800 copies. The original price was $2.25.

Contains: I — Excerpts from eighteen letters to Arthur R. Gledhill, pp. 3-11[1]. (Not printed elsewhere.)

---

[1] The figure eighteen is, it should be pointed out, an approximation. Some of these hitherto unpublished excerpts are given without dates, and it is sometimes not clear whether they constitute part of the same letter or of separate letters.

II — Excerpt from letter to Daniel Gregory Mason, pp. 13-14. (Originally published in *The Yale Review*, Vol. XXV, p. 863, June 1936.)

III — Excerpts from two letters to Amy Lowell, pp. 15-16. (Not printed elsewhere.)

IV — Excerpts from two letters to Arthur Davison Ficke, p. 19. (Not printed elsewhere.)

V — Letter to William Griffith, reproduced in facsimile, p. 17. (Not printed elsewhere.)

1947 *A House in Chicago*

By OLIVIA HOWARD DUNBAR / A HOUSE / IN CHICAGO / (drawing of Mrs. Harriet Moody's house) / THE UNIVERSITY OF CHICAGO PRESS / CHICAGO (dot) ILLINOIS /

Collation: [i]-viii + [1]-[288], as follows: [i] bastard title; [ii] blank; front. to face title: reproduction of photograph of Harriet Converse Tilden; [iii] title-page as above; [iv] publisher's address, notices of copyright, reservation of rights, date of publication, and press-work; [v] dedication; [vi] blank; vii-viii table of contents;[1] half-title to Part I; [2] blank; 3-269 text; [270] blank; [271] half-title to acknowledgments; [272] blank; 273 acknowledgments; [274] blank; [275] half-title to index; [276] blank; 277-[288] index; [288] colophon.

Issued in blue-green cloth. Stamped in gold on spine (in reverse: lettering to show cloth through gold, except for publisher's device): (rule) / (rule) / A / HOUSE /IN / CHICAGO / (diamond-shaped dot) / DUNBAR / (rule) / (rule) / (publisher's device) /. Top edge colored gold; fore and bottom edges trimmed. The leaves measure 21.4 by 14 cms.

Published 1947. The original price was $3.50.

Contains: I — Letters to Harriet Converse Moody, dated: approximately *November 1914*, pp. 108-109; and *December 1921*, p. 187. (Not printed elsewhere.)

II — Excerpts from letters to Harriet Converse Moody, dated approximately *October 1914*, p. 108; *1914*, pp. 111-112; *November*

1914, p. 113; *undated*, pp. 113-114; *1921*, p. 186; *June 1929*, p. 250. (Not printed elsewhere.)

1961 *Exiles and Fabrications*

EXILES and / FABRICATIONS / by / Winfield Townley Scott / *Doubleday & Company, Inc., Garden City, New York* / *1961* /

Collation: [1]-[216], as follows: [1] bastard title; [2] blank; [3] list of books by W. T. Scott; [4] blank; [5] title-page as above; [6] acknowledgments, notices of Library of Congress card number, copyright, reservation of rights, printing, and edition; [7] dedication; [8] blank; [9] contents; [10]-14 preface (signed: W. T. S. *22 December, 1960 Santa Fe, New Mexico*); [15] half-title; [16] blank; [17]-215 text; [216] blank.

Issued in gray cloth. Stamped in blue on front cover: EXILES AND FABRICATIONS / Winfield Townley Scott (signature) /. Stamped on spine, reading downwards: EXILES AND FABRICATIONS DOUBLEDAY (in red) / BY WINFIELD TOWNLEY SCOTT (in blue). Top edge colored blue; fore edge rough trimmed; bottom edge trimmed. The leaves measure 20.7 by 13.5 cms.

Published August 18, 1961. The original price was $3.95.

Contains: Three letters to the author, dated: *August 18, 1929*, *August 31, 1929*, and (in part) *October 7, 1934*; and an excerpt, dated: *August 12, 1932*, pp. 155-156, 162, 169, and 162. (Originally published in *The New Mexico Quarterly*, Vol. XXVI, pp. 161-178, Summer 1956.)

1969 *Edwin Arlington Robinson: Centenary Essays*

Edwin Arlington Robinson / *Centenary Essays* / *Edited by Ellsworth Barnard* / University of Georgia Press / *Athens* /

Collation: [i]-[xx] + [1]-192, as follows: [i] bastard title; [ii] blank; [iii] title-page as above; [iv] acknowledgments, notices of copyright, Library of Congress card and Standard Book numbers, press-work, printing, and binding; [v] contents; [vi] blank; [vii] preface (signed: E. B., Shelburne Falls, Massachusetts September

1969); [viii]-ix chronology; [x] Robinson's major publications
[xi]-xvii bibliography; [xviii] blank; [xix] half-title; [xx]
blank; [1]-183 text; [184]-186 notes on contributors; [187]-190
general index; [191]-192 indext to Robinson's works.

Issued in brown cloth, with dark brown backstrip. Stamped in gold
on front cover: Edwin / Arlington / Robinson / *Centenary* / *Essays* /
(rule) / *Edited by* / *Ellsworth Barnard* / (publisher's device) /.
Stamped in gold on spine, reading downwards: *Edwin Arlington Robin-*
son: Centenary Essays Barnard (rule) *Georgia* (last two words on two
lines separated by rule) /. All edges trimmed. The leaves measure
23.5 by 15.5 cms.

Published December 22, 1969. The original price was $6.50.

Contains: I — Excerpts from two letters to Josephine Preston
Peabody, dated: *February 1899*, p. 72 (Not printed elsewhere.)

II — Excerpts from eight letters to Jean (Mrs. Louis) Ledoux,
dated: *April 18, 1916, October 16, 1925, November 7, 1916, February*
2, 1921, July 30, 1916, August 26, 1917, August 3, 1925, and *February*
2, 1921, pp. 89, 91, 92, 94, 95, 95, 97, 98. (Not printed elsewhere.)

III — Excerpts from three letters to Louis Ledoux, dated: *April 18,*
1916, July 30, 1916, and *June 14, 1925*, pp. 92, 92, 101. (Not
printed elsewhere.)

IV — Excerpts from letter to Laura Richards, dated: *July 24, 1926*,
pp. 100. (Not printed elsewhere.)

V — Excerpts from letter to Lewis Isaacs, dated: *August 20,*
1924, p. 102. (Not printed elsewhere.)

1971 *Edwin Arlington Robinson: A Bio-Bibliography*

Edwin Arlington Robinson / *A Bio-Bibliography* / The H. Bacon
  Collamore Collection / in the Watkinson Library, Trinity College /
  Exhibited in the Trumbull Room / of the Watkinson Library /
  September–October 1969 / WATKINSON LIBRARY TRINITY
  COLLEGE HARTFORD, CONNECTICUT /

Collation: [i]-[viii] + 1-[48], as follows: [i] title-page as above;
  [ii] blank; iii preface; [iv] blank; v introduction (signed:
  JOHN WILLIAM PYE); [vi] blank; vii contents; [viii] blank; 1-41
  text; [42] blank; 43-44 index of work by E.A.R.; [45]-[48]
  blank.

Issued in orange wrappers, stapled. Printed in black on front
cover: Edwin Arlington Robinson / *A Bio-Bibliography* / WATKINSON
LIBRARY TRINITY COLLEGE HARTFORD, CONNECTICUT /. All
edged trimmed. The leaves measure 17.5 by 25.2 cms.

Not formally published. Issued January 21, 1971, in an edition of
500 copies. The edition was prepared (by John William Pye) for
private distribution, after which copes were priced at $3.75.

Contains: I — Excerpts from letters to Walter Hubbell, dated:
November 14, 1895, p. 2; *June 24, 1896*, p. 2; *December 16, 1896*, p. 3;
May 21, 1897, pp. 3-4. (Not printed elsewhere.)

II — "Twilight Song," 24 deleted lines from *Captain Craig*, 1902,
p. 5. (Not printed elsewhere; but the facsimile of the entire poem,
pp. [6]-[8], is also in *Letters to Edith Brower*, 1968, pp. 119-121.)

III — Excerpt from letter to Charles Eliot Norton, dated: *March
29, 1903*, p. 9. (Not printed elsewhere.)

IV — Excerpts from letter to William Stanley Braithwaite, dated:
January 6, 1916, p. 12. (Previous printing, see note below.)

V — Excerpt from letter to John G. Neihardt, dated: *January 24,
1914*, p. 13. (Not printed elsewhere.)

VI — Excerpts from letters to Samuel Roth, dated: *July 5, 1917*,
p. 15; *March 22, 1919*, p. 15; *June 17, 1919*, p. 16. (Previous printing,
see note below.)

VII — Excerpt from letter to Louis Van Ess, dated: *August 1,
1920*, p. 16. (Previous printing, see note below.)

VIII — Excerpt from letter to James R. Wells, dated: *August 28,
1928*, p. 19. (Previous printing, see note below.)

IX — Excerpts from letters to H. B. Collamore, dated: *January 19,
1929*, p. 19; *May 19, 1934*, p. 20; *December 12, 1928*, p. 20; *August 1,
1929*, pp. 20-21; *September 27, 1929*, p. 21; *October 11, 1930*, p. 21;
April 29, 1931, p. 22; *November 8, 1933*, p. 22; *November 20, 1933*,
p. 23. (Letter dater *December 12, 1928* not printed elsewhere; for
others, see note below.)

Note: Excerpt for letters indicated as not printed elsewhere, all of
the above letters had excerpts printed in *Edwin Arlington Robinson
(1969–1935): A Collection of His Works from the Library of Bacon
Collamore* (Hartford, 1936).

Among the items in the *Bio-Bibliography*, p. 38, is "An E. A. Robinson 'First,' " a clipping from the *Buffalo Evening News* (Buffalo), March 4, 1939, in which Howard G. Schmitt ascribes "Laziness," in *The Amateur* (Gardiner, Maine), 1886—see below, p. 29—to E. A. R. The Colby College copy of the magazine, however, has the initials E. G. M. after this article, for Robinson's friend, Ed Moore.

Under "Works Exhibited" are 148 items, and "Works Not Exhibited" are 191 items, including 78 letters (listed, with no excerpts) from E. A. R. and others. Robinson's inscriptions in 36 books, most of them not printed elsewhere, are also included in the book.

Part III. Work Originally Published in Periodicals

1886

BORES. *The Amateur* (Gardiner, Maine), pp. 10-11. [This is a 24-page pamphlet, with the sub-title, "Published by the Class of '88 of the Gardiner High School"—of which class Robinson was a member. The only date given is in an advertisement on page 4, which makes it clear that the pamphlet was issued sometime previous to July 1, 1887. Robinson's contribution is one of the fifteen unsigned essays, but its authorship has been established beyond any doubt. A copy of *The Amateur* was fortunately preserved by a member of the class, Harriet G. Andrews; and at the time of its appearance, she put at end of each of the fifteen articles the initials of the various authors. The ink used for this purpose has faded a little, but in *The Amateur* now in the Colby College Library, the letters "E. A. R." are plainly visible on page 11.] Not printed elsewhere. See Part V.

1890

ISAAC PITMAN. *The Phonographic World* (New York), Vol. V, p. 280, May. Reprinted in *Our Phonographic Poets*, 1904, pp. 79-80; and in *The Colophon* (New York), N. S. Vol. III, pp. 359-360, Summer 1938. See Part V, below.

1900

THE BALM OF CUSTOM. *The Daily Tribune* (New York), October
7, p. 8. Unsigned. Reprinted in *The New England Quarterly*
(Orono, Maine), Vol. XV, pp. 722-723, December 1942. See
Part V, below.

1916

[LETTER TO HARRY PERSONS TABER]. *The Cheshire Cat*
(Wilmington and Rehoboth, Delaware), July 15, 16, p. 8. Not
printed elsewhere.

1936

[TWO LETTERS TO WILLIAM LYON PHELPS]. *New York
Herald Tribune* (New York), November 13, pp. 14-15. Reprinted
in Mr. Phelp's *Autobiography with Letters*, 1939, pp. 696-697,
and in *Commemorative Tributes, The American Academy of
Arts and Letters* (New York), Academy Publication No. 95, 1939,
pp. 14-16.

[EXCERPT FROM LETTER TO HOUSTON MARTIN]. *The Yale
Review* (New Haven), Vol. XXVI, p. 294, December. Reprinted
in *Selected Letters of Edwin Arlington Robinson,* 1940, p. 174.

1937

[NINETEEN LETTERS TO DANIEL GREGORY MASON]. *The
Virginia Quarterly Review* (Charlottesville, Virginia), Vol.
XIII, pp. 54-69, Winter. Reprinted in part in Mr. Mason's *Music
in My Time*, 1938, pp. 83-89, 116-118, 121-123, 125-126.

[FIFTEEN LETTERS TO DANIEL GREGORY MASON]. *The
Virginia Quarterly Review* (Charlottesville, Virginia), Vol. XIII,
pp. 224-240, Spring. Reprinted in part in Mr. Mason's *Music
in My Time*, 1938, pp. 116-117, 124, 126-134.

[EXCERPTS FROM EIGHT LETTERS TO FLORENCE PELTIER].
The Mark Twain Quarterly (Webster Groves, Missouri), Vol.
I, pp. 13-14, Summer. Not printed elsewhere.

1938

[FOUR LETTERS TO PAUL LEMPERLY, ONE LETTER TO
R. H. STODDARD, ONE LETTER TO C. J. WEBER]. *The
Colby Mercury* (Waterville, Maine), Vol. VI, pp. 207-213,
November. Not printed elsewhere.

1939

[THREE LETTERS TO HENRY E. DUNNACK, TWO LETTERS
LETTERS TO ALANSON T. SCHUMANN]. *The Colby
Mercury* (Waterville, Maine), Vol. VI, pp. 282-284, December.
Not printed elsewhere.

1940

[EXCERPTS FROM TWELVE LETTERS TO AUGUSTUS AND
ALICE JORDAN]. *Lewiston Journal Magazine Section* (Lewiston
Maine), April 13, p. 8. Not printed elsewhere.

1941

THE NEXT "GREAT POET," INCOMPETENT AND CAPABLE
NOVELISTS, COMMERCIAL POTENCY AND LITERARY
SIGNIFICANCY. *The Colby Mercury* (Waterville, Maine), Vol.
VII, pp. 70-72, December. Reprinted from *The Daily Tribune*
(New York), these three pieces are probably not by Robinson.
See *The New England Quarterly* (Orono, Maine), Vol. XV
pp. 715-724, December 1942; and *The Colby Mercury*, March
1943, pp. 31-32.

1942

[FIVE LETTERS TO WILLIAM THOMAS WALSH]. *The Catholic
World* (New York), Vol. CLV, pp. 708-711, September. Not
printed elsewhere.
[FIVE LETTERS, AND EXCERPT FROM ONE LETTER, TO
EDMUND CLARENCE STEDMAN]. *The New England
Quarterly* (Orono, Maine), Vol. XV, pp. 716-720, December.
Not printed elsewhere.

1943

[TWO LETTERS TO ARTHUR R. GLEDHILL, ONE LETTER TO
EDWIN MARKHAM, ONE LETTER TO ESTHER W.
BATES]. *Colby Library Quarterly* (Waterville, Maine), Series I,
pp. 9-12, January. Not printed elsewhere.

[EXCERPTS FROM TWO LETTERS TO EDITH BROWER]. *Colby
Library Quarterly* (Waterville, Maine), Series I, p. 30, March.
Reprinted in full in *Letters to Edith Brower*, 1968, pp. 160,
171-172.

1944

[ONE LETTER TO CARL J. WEBER, ONE LETTER TO DR. LOUIS
DICKSTEIN, ONE LETTER TO HERBERT C. LIBBY].
Colby Library Quarterly (Waterville, Maine), Series I, pp. 84-85,
January. [The letter to Mr. Weber originally printed in *The
Colby Mercury*, November 1938, p. 213; the other letters not
printed elsewhere.]

1947

[LETTER TO EDMUND R. BROWN]. *Colby Library Quarterly*
(Waterville, Maine), Series II, p. 43, August. Not printed
elsewhere.

[IDEALIST?: AN OCTAVE]. *Colby Library Quarterly* (Waterville,
Maine), Series II, p. 13, February. Reprinted in the *Letters to
Edith Brower*, 1968, p. 36. See Part V, below.

1951

[BROADWAY: A POEM]. *American Literature* (Durham, North
Carolina), Vol. XXII, p. 488, January. Not printed elsewhere.
See Part V.

[TEN LETTERS TO WILLIAM VAUGHN MOODY]. *American
Literature* (Durham, North Carolina), Vol. XXIII, pp. 174-187,
May. Not printed elsewhere.

1954

[TWO LETTERS TO WILLIAM ALLAN NEILSON]. *The New England Quarterly* (Brunswick, Maine), Vol. XXVII, p. 258, June. Not printed elsewhere.

1956

[THREE LETTERS, AND EXCERPT FROM ONE LETTER, TO WINFIELD TOWNLEY SCOTT]. *The New Mexico Quarterly* (Albuquerque), Vol. XXVI, pp. 163, 170, 177-178, Summer. Reprinted in Mr. Scott's *Exiles and Fabrications*, 1961, pp. 155-156, 162, 169.

1960

[LETTER TO WAITMAN BARBE]. *Colby Library Quarterly* (Waterville, Maine), Series V, p. 164, September. Not printed elsewhere.
[NOTES TO ROBINSON'S NIECES]. *Colby Library Quarterly* (Waterville, Maine), Series V, pp. 195-203, December. Not printed elsewhere.

1962

[THIRTEEN LETTERS TO HARRIET MONROE]. *Modern Philology* (Chicago), Vol. LX, pp. 32, 34-39, August. One reproduced in facsimile in Miss Monroe's *A Poet's Life*, 1938, between pp. 254-255, and printed, in part, in *Poetry*, Vol. XLVII, p. 34, October 1935. Others not printed elsewhere.
[EXCERPTS FROM SIX LETTERS TO EDITH BROWER]. *Colby Library Quarterly*, Series VI, pp. 181-183, December. Reprinted in full in *Letters to Edith Brower*, 1968, pp. 130-140, 152-153.

1963

[EXCERPTS FROM SIX LETTERS TO EDITH BROWER]. *Victorian Newsletter* (New York), No. 23, pp. 19-21, Spring. Printed in full in *Letters to Edith Brower*, 1968, pp. 52, 70, 93, 101, 169, 195.

[EXCERPTS FROM TWENTY-SEVEN LETTERS TO EDITH BROWER]. *Colby Library Quarterly* (Waterville, Maine), Series VI, pp. 235-244, June. Printed in full in *Letters to Edith Brower,* pp. 20-199, *passim.*

[EXCERPTS FROM THREE LETTERS TO EDITH BROWER]. *American Notes & Queries* (New Haven, Connecticut), Vol. II, pp. 35-36, November. Printed in full in *Letters to Edith Brower,* 1968, pp. 193, 194, 196.

1964

[LETTER TO JAMES BARSTOW]. *The New England Quarterly* (Brunswick, Maine), Vol. XXXVII, pp. 390-392, September. Not printed elsewhere.

1967

[THREE LETTERS TO CARL W. MARR]. *Colby Library Quarterly* (Waterville, Maine). Series VII, pp. 516-517, 519-520, 525, December. Not printed elsewhere.

1969

[MR. FLOOD'S PARTY: VARIANT CONCLUDING STANZA]. *English Language Notes* (Boulder, Colorado), Vol. VII p. 57, September. Not printed elsewhere.

1970

[EXCERPTS FROM LETTER TO LEWIS ISAACS, NINE LETTERS TO HENRY CABOT LODGE]. *The New England Quarterly* (Brunswick, Maine), Vol. XLIII, pp. 115-123, March. Not printed elsewhere.

Part IV. Biographicaland Critical Material Dealing with Robinson

A. Books

1924

THE WORKS OF THEODORE ROOSEVELT. MEMORIAL EDITION. VOL. XIV [LITERARY ESSAYS]. New York: Charles Scribner's Sons. 595 pp. *The Children of the Night*, pp. 360-364. [Originally published in *The Outlook*, New York, Vol. LXXX, pp. 913-914, August 12, 1905.]

1926

PANORAMA DE LA LITTÉRATURE AMÉRICAINE CONTEMPORAINE, by Régis Michaud. Paris: Kra. 275 pp. [*E. A. Robinson*] pp. 184-186.

ANTHOLOGY OF MAGAZINE VERSE FOR 1926, edited by William Stanley Braithwaite. Boston: B. J. Brimmer Company. 897 pp. In article entitled *Poetry of New England*, by Jessie B[elle] Rittenhouse, pp. 12-16.

CURRENT REVIEWS, edited by Lewis Worthington Smith. New York: Henry Holt & Company. 388 pp. *Dionysus in Doubt*, by Percy A[dams] Hutchison, pp. 308-314. [Originally published in *The New York Times Book Review*, New York, March 29, 1925, p. 5.]

1927

UNDERSTANDING GREAT POEMS, by Samuel Marion Lowden. Harrisburg, Pennsylvania: Handy Book Corporation. 340 pp. *The Gift of God*, pp. 265-273.

MONEY WRITES!, by Upton Sinclair. New York: Albert & Charles Boni. 227 pp. *Choose Your Poet*, pp. 152-155.
THE WINGED HORSE, by Joseph Auslander and Frank Ernest Hill. New York: Doubleday, Page & Company. *Under Steam and Stone*, pp. 405-407.

1929

TWENTIETH CENTURY POETRY, by John Drinkwater. Boston: Houghton Mifflin Company. *Edwin Arlington Robinson*, pp. 316-317.
CONTEMPORARY AMERICAN LITERATURE, by John Matthews Manly, Edith Rickert, and Fred B. Millett. New York: Harcourt, Brace and Company. *Poets of New England: Robinson and Frost*, pp. 47-48. [See also 1922 edition, *Edwin Arlington Robinson*, pp. 130-132.]

1930

THE SONNET IN AMERICAN LITERATURE, by Lewis G. Sterner. Philadelphia [University of Pennsylvania]. [*Edwin Arlington Robinson*], pp. 75-77.

1931

LE ROMAN DE TRISTAN ET ISEUT DANS LA LITTÉRATURE ANGLO-AMÉRICAINE AU XIXe ET AU XXe SIÈCLES, by Maurice Halperin. Paris: Jouve & Cie. 146 pp. *La vérité psychologique*, pp. 107-119.
AMERICAN HUMOR, by Constance Rourke. New York: Harcourt, Brace and Company. 324 pp. [*E. A. Robinson*] pp. 271-274.
LIVING AUTHORS: A BOOK OF BIOGRAPHIES, by Dilly Tante [Stanley Kunitz]. New York: The H. W. Wilson Company. 466 pp. *Edwin Arlington Robinson*, pp. 344-346.

1933

THE GREAT TRADITION, by Granville Hicks. New York: The Macmillan Company. 317 pp. [*E. A. Robinson*] pp. 242-245.

A STUDY OF THE DRAMATIC MONOLOGUE IN AMERICAN AND
CONTINENTAL LITERATURE, by Ina Beth Sessions. San Antonio:
Alamo Printing Company. 197 pp. [*E. A. Robinson*] pp. 108-116.

1934

MY HOUSE OF LIFE: AN AUTOBIOGRAPHY, by Jessie B. Rittenhouse.
Boston and New York: Houghton Mifflin Company. [*Edwin
Arlington Robinson*] pp. 211-212, 282.

SOUCASNÁ LITERATURA SPOJENYCH STÁTU, by Otakar Vačadlo.
Prague: Vydal Jan Laichter. 223 pp. *Edwin Arlington Robinson*,
pp. 37-40.

1935

PANORAMA DE LA LITERATURA NORTEAMERICANA (1600-1935), by
Jose Antonio Ramos. Mexico: Ediciones Botas. 265 pp. [*E. A.
Robinson*] pp. 170, 173-175.

WHAT IS AMERICAN LITERATURE? by Carl Van Doren. New York:
William Morrow and Company. 128 pp. [*E. A. Robinson*]
pp. 106-110.

1936

THE CONCEPT OF NATURE IN NINETEENTH-CENTURY ENGLISH
POETRY, by Joseph Warren Beach. New York: The Macmillan
Company. 618 pp. [*E. A. Robinson*] pp. 538-539.

MAJOR AMERICAN POETS, edited by Harry Hayden Clark. New York,
etc.: American Book Company. 964 pp. *Edwin Arlington Robinson*,
pp. 938-947.

THE EDWIN ARLINGTON ROBINSON MEMORIAL [by Hermann
Hagedorn]. Gardiner, Maine [Privately printed]. 36 pp.

A BIBLIOGRAPHY OF EDWIN ARLINGTON ROBINSON, by Charles Beacher
Hogan. New Haven: Yale University Press. [xiv], 222 pp.
Contains: First publication in book form of five poems, "Thalia,"
"The Galley Race," " 'I Make No Measure of the Words They
Say,' " "Shooting Stars," and "Octave," pp. 167-175; and ten prose
pieces, "A New England Poet," "From Mr. Robinson," Letter to

Alice Hunt Bartlett, "Pleasing Letter from Edwin Arlington
Robinson Regarding the New England Sonnet," "MacDowell's
Legacy to Art," Excerpt from Letter to The Macmillan Company,
"Vachel Lindsay," Letter to Edna Davis Romig, Excerpt from
Letter to Albert O. Bassuk, and Letter to Patience B. Clarke,
pp. 176-186. [The *Bibliography* has been reprinted by The
Folcroft Press, Folcroft, Pennsylvania.]

AN INTRODUCTION TO POETRY, by Jay B. Hubbell and John O. Beaty.
New York: The Macmillan Company. [*Edwin Arlington
Robinson*] passim (20 references and 15 poems quoted). [See also
1923 edition, pp. 11, 188, 210-211, 290, 379, 406, 421.]

MOVERS AND SHAKERS, by Mabel Dodge Luhan. New York: Harcourt,
Brace and Company, 542 pp. [*E. A. Robinson*] pp. 43, 74,
123-139, 444.

ELEGY FOR ROBINSON [verse], by Winfield Townley Scott, New York:
The Bachrach Press, 16 pp.

A HISTORY OF AMERICAN LETTERS, by Walter Fuller Taylor. New
York, etc.: American Book Company. 678 pp. *Edwin Arlington
Robinson (1869-1935)*, pp. 339-347.

MODERN AMERICAN POETRY, edited by Louis Untermeyer. New York:
Harcourt, Brace and Company. 654 pp. *Edwin Arlington Robinson*,
pp. 139-143.

1937

NEXT DOOR TO A POET, by Rollo Walter Brown. New York, etc.:
D. Appleton-Century Co. 98 pp.

A BIBLIOGRAPHY OF THE WRITINGS AND CRITICISMS OF EDWIN
ARLINGTON ROBINSON, by Lillian Lippincott. Boston: The F. W.
Faxon Company. 86 pp.

I HEAR AMERICA. . . , by Vernon Loggins. New York: Thomas Y.
Crowell Company. 378 pp. *Edwin Arlington Robinson*, pp. 51-60.

LITERARY OPINION IN AMERICA, edited by Morton Dauwen Zabel.
New York, etc.: Harper & Brothers. 637 pp. *Robinson*,
pp. 397-406. (Originally published in *The Commonweal*, New
York, Vol. XVII, pp. 436-438, February 15, 1933, and in *Poetry*,
Chicago, Vol. XLVI, pp. 157-162, June 1935).

1938

NEW POETRY OF NEW ENGLAND, by Robert P[eter] Tristram Coffin. Baltimore: The Johns Hopkins Press, 148 pp. [*E. A. Robinson*] pp. 17-19, 25-50, 73, 77-89, 108-109, 132, 136-137, 141-145.

EDWIN ARLINGTON ROBINSON, by Hermann Hagedorn. New York: The Macmillan Company. 402 pp.

MUSIC IN MY TIME, by Daniel Gregory Mason. New York: The Macmillan Company. 409 pp. [*E. A. Robinson*] pp. 82-89, 116-118, 121-134, 140.

THE WORLD I SAW, by Theodore Maynard. Milwaukee: The Bruce Publishing Company. 313 pp [*E. A. Robinson*] pp. 232-238.

POETS AT PRAYER, by Sister Mary James Power. New York, etc.: Sheed & Ward. 214 pp. *Edwin Arlington Robinson: The First of the Seekers*, pp. 71-82.

1939

MY TILBURY TOWN, by James S[tewart] Barstow. [New York: Privately printed.] 11 pp.

THE FRIENDS [verse], by James Norman Hall. Muscatine, Iowa: The Prairie Press. 34 pp.

THE SMALL TOWN IN AMERICAN LITERATURE, by Ima Honaker Herron. Durham, North Carolina: Duke University Press. 477 pp. [*E. A. Robinson*] pp. 130-136.

AUTOBIOGRAPHY WITH LETTERS, by William Lyon Phelps. New York, etc.: Oxford University Press. 986 pp. *Edwin Arlington Robinson*, pp. 693-698 (Originally published in *New York Herald Tribune*, New York, November 13, 1936, pp. 14-15).

FROM ANOTHER WORLD, by Louis Untermeyer. New York: Harcourt, Brace and Company. 394 pp. [*E. A. Robinson*] pp. 222-227.

1940

NEW ENGLAND: INDIAN SUMMER 1865-1915, by Van Wyck Brooks. [New York:] E. P. Dutton & Co., Inc. 557 pp. [*E. A. Robinson*] pp. 491-499, 527.

PHILOSOPHY IN THE POETRY OF EDWIN ARLINGTON ROBINSON, by Estelle Kaplan. New York: Columbia University Press. 162 pp.

TWENTIETH CENTURY AUTHORS: A BIOGRAPHICAL DICTIONARY OF
MODERN LITERATURE, edited by Stanley J. Kunitz and Howard
Haycraft. New York: The H. W. Wilson Company. 1577 pp.
Robinson, Edwin Arlington, pp. 1185-1186. [See also FIRST
SUPPLEMENT, 1955, p. 834.]

CONTEMPORARY AMERICAN AUTHORS, by Fred B. Millett. New York:
Harcourt, Brace & Company. 716 pp. *Edwin Arlington
Robinson*, pp. 548-554.

HARVARD DAYS WITH EDWIN ARLINGTON ROBINSON, by James L[ibby]
Tryon [Waterville, Maine: Privately printed.] 16 pp.

EDWIN ARLINGTON ROBINSON, by Dorothy Livingston Ulrich.
[Hartford: Privately printed.] 7 pp. (Originally published in
Avocations, New York, Vol. II, pp. 248-253, June 1938.)

NEW POETS FROM OLD, by Henry W[illis] Wells. New York: Columbia
University Press. 356 pp.[*E. A. Robinson*] pp. 90-97, 316-320.

1942

AMERICAN ACADEMY OF ARTS AND LETTERS: COMMEMORATIVE
TRIBUTES, 1905-1941. New York: The Academy.
Edwin Arlington Robinson, by William Lyon Phelps, pp. 323-328.

1943

AMERICAN IDEALISM, by Floyd Stovall. Norman: University of
Oklahoma Press. *Robinson and Frost*, pp. 167-186.

THE AMERICAN WAY OF POETRY, by Henry W. Wells. New York:
Columbia University Press. *New England Conscience*, pp. 89-105.
[Reprinted by Russell and Russell, New York, 1965.]

1944

EDWIN ARLINGTON ROBINSON AT COLBY COLLEGE. Waterville, Maine:
Colby College Library. 4 pp.

EDWIN ARLINGTON ROBINSON AND HIS MANUSCRIPTS, by Esther
Willard Bates. Colby College Monograph No. 11. Waterville,
Maine: Colby College Library. 32 pp.

THE DICTIONARY OF AMERICAN BIOGRAPHY, VOL. XXI. New York: Charles Scribner's Sons. *Edwin Arlington Robinson*, by Louis V. Ledoux, pp. 632-634.

1945

ONE WORD AFTER ANOTHER, by Warren Sturgis McCulloch. Chicago: Chicago Literary Club. 28 pp. [Tribute to Edwin Arlington Robinson, read before the club on March 12, 1945.]

1946

A HISTORY OF AMERICAN POETRY (1900-1940), by Horace Gregory and Marya Zaturenska. New York: Harcourt, Brace and Company. *La Comédie Humaine of E. A. Robinson*, pp. 107-132.

EDWIN ARLINGTON ROBINSON, by Yvor Winters. The Makers of Modern Literature [Series]. Norfolk, Connecticut: New Directions Books, [vi], 162 pp. [The chapter, "The Shorter Poems," was reprinted in Francis Murphy, *A Collection* . . . See 1970, below.]

1947

A HOUSE IN CHICAGO, by Olivia Howard Dunbar [Mrs. Ridgely Torrence]. Chicago: University of Chicago Press. viii, 288 pp.

1948

COLLECTED ESSAYS OF JOHN PEALE BISHOP, edited with an Introduction by Edmund Wilson. New York: Charles Scribner's Sons. *Intelligence of Poets*, pp. 263-269.

ANTHOLOGIE DE LA POÉSIE AMÉRICAINE CONTEMPORAINE, by Maurice le Breton. Paris: Éditions Denoël. 346 pp. [*E. A. Robinson*] pp. 40-41.

THE CHRIST OF THE POETS, by Edwin Mims. Nashville, Tennessee: Abington-Cokesbury Press. *Contemporary Poets: Edwin Arlington Robinson*, pp. 222-224.

EDWIN ARLINGTON ROBINSON, by Emery Neff. The American Men of Letters Series. New York: William Sloane Associates. xviii, 286 pp.

42

LITERARY HISTORY OF THE UNITED STATES, edited by Robert E.
Spiller, Willard Thorp, Thomas H. Johnson, and Henry Seidel
Canby. New York: The Macmillan Company. *Edwin Arlington
Robinson*, by Stanley T. Williams, [Vol. II] pp. 1157-1170.
[See also Thomas H. Johnson's bibliography in Vol. III.]
ON THE LIMITS OF POETRY: SELECTED ESSAYS, 1928-1948, by Allen
Tate. New York: William Morrow. *Edwin Arlington Robinson*
["*Talifer*"], pp. 358-364.

1949

CHILMARK MISCELLANY, by Van Wyck Brooks. New York: E. P.
Dutton. *Edwin Arlington Robinson*, pp. 245-261.
COSMIC OPTIMISM, by Frederick William Conner. Gainesville:
University of Florida Press. [*Edwin Arlington Robinson*],
pp. 365-374.
ROBINSON'S SONNETS, by George Mitchell. Ph. D. Thesis. Philadelphia:
Temple University.

1950

THE AMERICAN MIND, by Henry Steele Commager. New Haven:
Yale University Press. *The Traditionalists*, pp. 141-161.
THE LIBRARY OF EDWIN ARLINGTON ROBINSON: A DESCRIPTIVE
CATALOGUE, compiled by James Humphry, III. Colby College
Monograph. No. 19. Waterville, Maine: Colby College Press.
52 pp.
READING POETRY, by Fred B. Millett. New York: Harper & Brothers.
["*Flammonde*"] p. 64.
SOME MODERN AMERICAN POETS, by James Granville Southworth.
New York: The Macmillan Company. *Edwin Arlington Robinson*,
pp. 28-41.
THE HEEL OF ELOHIM: SCIENCE AND VALUES IN MODERN AMERICAN
POETRY, by H. H. Waggoner. Norman: University of Oklahoma
Press. *E. A. Robinson: The Cosmic Chill*, pp. 18-40. Revised from
The New England Quarterly, Vol. XIII, pp. 65-84, March 1940.
Reprinted in Francis Murphy, *A Collection* . . . see 1970, below.

1951

Poems in Process, by Phyllis Bartlett. New York: Oxford University Press. [*Edwin Arlington Robinson*]. pp. 104-106.

Achievement in American Poetry 1900-1950, by Louise Bogan. Chicago: Henry Regnery Company. [*Edwin Arlington Robinson*]. pp. 19-22. [Paperback edition, 1962, pp. 15-19.]

Breve Storia della Letteratura Americana, by Silvio Policardi. Milano, Varese: Istituto Edioriale Cisalpino. *Edwin Arlington Robinson (1869-1935)*, pp. 218-219.

Acres of Flint: Writers of Rural New England, 1870-1900, by Perry D. Westbrook. Washington: The Scarecrow Press. *E. A. Robinson,* pp. 111-113. See also p. 181.

1952

Edwin Arlington Robinson: A Critical Study, by Ellsworth Barnard. New York: The Macmillan Company. [xvi], 318 pp.

Das lyrische Werk Edwin Arlington Robinsons, by Alfred Baumgärtner. Ph.D. Thesis, Mainz University.

Poetry In Our Time, by Babette Deutsch. New York: Henry Holt and Company. *Glove of a Neighborhood,* pp. 55-78.

Poetry as Experience, by Norman C. Stageberg and Wallace Anderson. New York: American Book Company. [*"Richard Cory"*] pp. 189-192.

The Shores of Light: A Literary Chronicle of the Twenties and Thirties, by Edmund Wilson. New York: Farrar, Straus and Young, Inc. *Mr. E. A. Robinson's Moonlight,* pp. 36-38. From *The Dial* (New York), Vol. LXXIV, pp. 515-517, May 1923.

1954

Panorama de la littérature contemporaine aux États-Unis, by John Brown. Nrf. Paris: Librarie Gallimard. *Edwin Arlington Robinson (1869-1935)*, pp. 260-261.

Edwin Arlington Robinson: The Literary Background of a Traditional Poet, by Edwin S. Fussell. Berkeley and Los

Angeles: University of California Press. [xii], 211 pp. [The
chapter, "One Kind of Traditional Poet," was reprinted in
Francis Murphy, *A Collection* . . . See 1970, below.]
THE STRENUOUS AGE IN AMERICAN LITERATURE, by Grant C. Knight.
Chapel Hill: The University of North Carolina Press. [*Edwin
Arlington Robinson*] pp. 74-75, 209-210.
ARTICLES ON AMERICAN LITERATURE, 1900-1950, by Lewis Leary.
Durham, North Carolina: Duke University Press. [*Edwin
Arlington Robinson*] pp. 258-263.
KING ARTHUR TODAY, by Nathan C. Starr. Gainesville, Florida:
University of Florida Press.
SIXTY AMERICAN POETS 1896-1944, SELECTED, WITH PREFACE AND
CRITICAL NOTES, by Allen Tate. Revised Edition. Washington:
The Library of Congress. *Edwin Arlington Robinson*, pp. 107-113.

1955

THE CYCLE OF AMERICAN LITERATURE: AN ESSAY IN HISTORICAL
CRITICISM, by Robert E. Spiller. New York: The Macmillan
Company. *A Problem in Dynamics: Adams, Norris, Robinson*,
pp. 184-210. [Reprinted New York: The New American Library,
1957. See pp. 143-161.]
MAKERS OF THE MODERN WORLD, by Louis Untermeyer. New York:
Simon and Schuster. *Edwin Arlington Robinson*, pp. 399-404.

1956

HISTORIA DE LA LITERATURA NORTEAMERICANA, by Concha Zardoya.
Barcelona, etc.: Editorial Labor, S.A. *Edwin Arlington Robinson*,
pp. 320-323.

1957

AMERICAN WRITING TODAY: ITS INDEPENDENCE AND VIGOR,
edited by Allan Angoff. The Times, London, Literary Supplement.
New York: New York University Press. *Edwin Arlington
Robinson*, pp. 354-356. [On the *Collected Poems*. Reprinted
from *The Times Literary Supplement*, September 17, 1954.]

1958

COLLECTED CRITICISM OF CONRAD AIKEN FROM 1916 TO THE
PRESENT: A REVIEWER'S ABC, by Conrad Aiken. New York:
Meridian Books. *Edwin Arlington Robinson*, pp. 333-346.
[Reprinted in Francis Murphy, *A Collection* . . . See 1970, below.]

1959

COLLECTED ESSAYS, by Allen Tate. Denver: Alan Swallow. *Edwin
Arlington Robinson*, pp. 358-364. [Reprinted in *Essays of Four
Decades*, by Allen Tate (Chicago: Swallow Press, Inc., 1969),
pp. 341-347.]

1960

IN PURSUIT OF POETRY, by Robert Hillyer. New York [etc.]: McGraw-
Hill Book Company, Inc. [*Edward* [*sic*] *Arlington Robinson*]
pp. 25, 63-64, 79-80, 82-87, 113, 146, 163, 187, 189.
A LIBRARY OF LITERARY CRITICISM: MODERN AMERICAN LITERATURE,
compiled and edited by Dorothy Nyren. New York: Frederick
Ungar Publishing Co. *Robinson, Edwin Arlington (1869-1935)*,
pp. 404-407.
THE MODERN POETS: A CRITICAL INTRODUCTION, by M. L. Rosenthal.
New York: Oxford University Press. *Rival Idioms: The Great
Generation: Robinson and Frost*, pp. 104-112.
AMERICAN WRITING IN THE TWENTIETH CENTURY, by Willard
Thorp. Cambridge: Harvard University Press. [*E. A. Robinson*]
pp. 38-42.

1961

THE CONTINUITY OF AMERICAN POETRY, by Roy Harvey Pearce.
Princeton: Princeton University Press. *The Old Poetry and the
New: 2. Robinson*, pp. 256-269.
EXILES AND FABRICATIONS, by Winfield Townley Scott. Garden City,
New York: Doubleday and Company, Inc. *To See Robinson*,
pp. 154-170.

LEXIKON DER WELTLITERATUR IM 20. JAHRHUNDERT. Freiburg, Basel,
Wien: Herder. *Robinson, Edwin Arlington*, by Ray Smith, Vol.
II, col. 758-759.

1962

EDWIN ARLINGTON ROBINSON, by Louis Coxe. University of Minnesota
Pamphlets on American Writers No. 17. Minneapolis:
University of Minnesota Press. 48 pp.
SUPPLEMENT to Thomas H. Johnson, BIBLIOGRAPHY: LITERARY
HISTORY OF THE UNITED STATES, by Richard M. Ludwig.
New York: The Macmillan Company. *Edwin Arlington Robinson*,
pp. 705-708.
RELIGIOUS TRENDS IN ENGLISH POETRY; VOLUME V: 1880-1920,
GODS OF A CHANGING POETRY, by Hoxie Neale Fairchild.
New York and London: Columbia University Press.
Realists, pp. 238-243.

1963

THE INCLUSIVE FLAME: STUDIES IN AMERICAN POETRY, by Glauco
Cambon. Bloomington: Indiana University Press. *Edwin Arlington
Robinson: Knight of the Grail*, pp. 53-78.
POETRY IN OUR TIME: A CRITICAL SURVEY OF POETRY IN THE
ENGLISH-SPEAKING WORLD 1900 - 1960, by Babette Deutsch.
Second edition, revised and enlarged. Garden City, New York:
Doubleday & Company, Inc. *The Glove of a Neighborhood*,
pp. 59-84.
THE CONCISE ENCYCLOPEDIA OF ENGLISH AND AMERICAN POETS AND
POETRY, edited by Stephen Spender and Donald Hall. New York:
Hawthorn Books, Inc. *Robinson, Edwin Arlington*, by E. N. W.
Mottram, pp. 275-276.
EDWIN ARLINGTON ROBINSON: A REAPPRAISAL, WITH A BIBLIOGRAPHY
AND A LIST OF MATERIALS IN THE EDWIN ARLINGTON
ROBINSON EXHIBIT ON DISPLAY AT THE LIBRARY OF CONGRESS,
APRIL 15 TO JULY 15, 1963, by Louis Untermeyer. Washington:
Library of Congress [vi], 39 pp.

A Dial Miscellany, edited with an Introduction by William
Wasserstrom. Syracuse: Syracuse University Press. *A Bird's-Eye
View of E. A. Robinson,* by Amy Lowell, pp. 75-87.

1964

Sound and Form in Modern Poetry: A Study of Prosody from
Thomas Hardy to Robert Lowell, by Harvey Gross. Ann
Arbor: University of Michigan Press. *Edwin Arlington Robinson
and Robert Frost,* pp. 63-67.

New Poetry of New England, by Robert P. Tristram Coffin. New
York: Russell & Russell. [*Edwin Arlington Robinson*] pp. 17-19,
25-50, 73, 77-89, 108-109, 132, 136-137, 141-145. [Originally
published, Johns Hopkins Press, 1938.]

After the Genteel Tradition: American Writers, 1910-1930,
by Malcolm Cowley. Revised and enlarged. Carbondale:
Southern Illinois University Press. *Edwin Arlington Robinson,*
pp. 28-36.

Review Notes and Study Guide to Twentieth Century British
and American Poets, by Eve Leoff. New York: Monarch Press.
E. A. Robinson, pp. 39-41.

1965

The Ferment of Realism: American Literature, 1884-1919, by
Warner Berthoff. New York: The Free Press, *The "New" Poetry:
Robinson and Frost,* pp. 263-272. [Reprinted in Francis Murphy,
A Collection . . . See 1970, below.]

Connoisseurs of Chaos: Ideas of Order in Modern American
Poetry, by Denis Donoghue. New York: The Macmillan Company.
Edwin Arlington Robinson, J. V. Cunningham, Robert Lowell,
pp. 129-159.

Oxford Companion to American Literature, by James D. Hart.
Fourth Edition. New York: Oxford University Press. *Robinson,
Edwin Arlington (1869-1935),* pp. 718-719; also *Avon's Harvest,
Ben Jonson Entertains a Man from Stratford, The Book of
Annandale, Captain Craig, Cassandra, Cavender's House, Demos
and Dionysus, Dionysus in Doubt, Flammonde, King Jasper,*

Lancelot, The Man Against the Sky, The Man Who Died Twice, Matthias at the Door, Merlin, Miniver Cheevy, Rahel to Varnhagen, Rembrandt to Rembrandt, Roman Bartholow, Talifer, Tilbury Town, and *Tristram.*

MY LIFE IN PUBLISHING, by Harold S. Latham. New York: E. P. Dutton & Co. Inc. *Edwin Arlington Robinson,* pp. 42-47.

STUDIES IN AMERICAN LITERATURE: WHITMAN, EMERSON, MELVILLE AND OTHERS, by Egbert S. Oliver. New Delhi: Eurasia Publishing House. *Robinson's Dark-Hill-to-Climb Image.* [Reprinted from *Literary Criticism* (Mysore, India), Vol. III, pp. 36-52, Summer 1959.]

UOMINI E OMBRE, by Edwin Arlington Robinson, translated [into Italian] by Alfredo Giuliani. Milano: Mondadori. 168 pp. 1600 lira.

WHERE THE LIGHT FALLS: A PORTRAIT OF EDWIN ARLINGTON ROBINSON, by Chard Powers Smith. New York: The Macmillan Company; London: Collier-Macmillan Limited. 420 pp.

AMERICAN LITERARY MASTERS, general editor, Charles R. Anderson. New York [etc.]: Holt, Rinehart and Winston. *Introduction* to Edwin Arlington Robinson, by Carl F. Strauch, II, 507-516; 23 Robinson poems, with annotations, pp. 516-561; Reading Suggestions and Biography, pp. 561-563.

AMERICAN LITERARY SCHOLARSHIP: AN ANNUAL / 1963, edited by James Woodress. Durham, North Carolina. *E. A. Robinson,* by Charles T. Davis, pp. 170-172.

1966

STUDIES IN LANGUAGE AND LITERATURE IN HONOUR OF MARGARET SCHLAUCH, edited by Mieczyslaw Brahmer, Stanislaw Helsztyński, and Julian Krzyzanowski. Warsaw: Państwowe Wydawnictwo Naukowe. *Edwin Arlington Robinson and Arthurian Tradition,* by John H. Fisher, pp. 117-131.

AMERICANA NORVEGICA: NORWEGIAN CONTRIBUTIONS TO AMERICAN STUDIES, Vol. I, edited by Sigmund Skard and Henry H. Wasser. Oslo: Glydendal Norsk Forlag; Philadelphia: University of

Pennsylvania Press. *E. A. Robinson: "Eros Turannos," a Critical Survey*, by Sigmund Skard, pp. 286-330.

THE EXPICATOR CYCLOPEDIA, Vol. I, Modern Poetry, edited by Charles Child Walcutt and J. Edwin Whitesell. Chicago: Quadrangle Books. *Robinson*, pp. 245-262. [Explications of 16 poems reprinted from *The Explicator*.]

THE NEW ENGLAND CONSCIENCE, by Austin Warren. Ann Arbor: University of Michigan Press. *Edwin Arlington Robinson*, pp. 181-193.

THE AMERICAN 1890s: LIFE AND TIMES OF A LOST GENERATION, by Larzer Ziff. New York: The Viking Press. *In and Out of Laodicea: The Harvard Poets and Edwin Arlington Robinson*, pp. 306-333.

1967

EDWIN ARLINGTON ROBINSON: A CRITICAL INTRODUCTION, by Wallace L. Anderson. Riverside Studies in Literature. Boston: Houghton Mifflin Company, 1967; Cambridge: Harvard University Press, 1968. xvi, 175 pp. [Selected Bibliography, pp. 155-165.]

HARVESTS OF CHANGE: AMERICAN LITERATURE 1865-1914, by Jay Martin. Englewood Cliffs, New Jersey: Prentice-Hall, Inc. *Edwin Arlington Robinson*, pp. 152-159.

E. A. R., by Laura E. Richards. New York: Russell & Russell. [Originally published, Harvard University Press, 1936.]

EDWIN ARLINGTON ROBINSON: A POETRY OF THE ACT, by W. R. Robinson. Cleveland, Ohio: The Press of Western Reserve University. 183 pp. [The chapter, "The Alienated Self," was reprinted in Francis Murphy, *A Collection* . . . See 1970, below.]

ESSAYS ON AMERICAN LITERATURE IN HONOR OF JAY B. HUBBELL, edited by Clarence Gohdes. Durham: Duke University Press. *Edwin Arlington Robinson in Perspective*, by Floyd Stovall, pp. 241-258.

AMERICAN LITERARY SCHOLARSHIP: AN ANNUAL / 1965, edited by James Woodress. Durham, North Carolina: Duke University Press. *Edwin Arlington Robinson*, by Ann Stanford, pp. 208-210.

1968

THE READER'S ADVISER: A GUIDE TO THE BEST IN LITERATURE, edited
by Winifred F. Courtney. 11th Edition, revised and enlarged.
New York and London: R. R. Bowker Company. *Robinson, Edwin
Arlington, 1869-1935*, p. 196.

BABEL TO BYZANTIUM: POETS AND POETRY NOW, by James Dickey.
New York: Farrar, Straus and Giroux. *Edwin Arlington Robinson*,
pp. 209-230.

EDWIN ARLINGTON ROBINSON, by Hoyt C. Franchere. Twayne's United
States Authors Series No. 137. New York: Twayne Publishers,
Inc. 161 pp.

EDWIN ARLINGTON ROBINSON, by Emery Neff. New York: Russell &
Russell. [Originally published, William Sloane Associates, 1948.]

ESSAYS OF FOUR DECADES, by Allen Tate. Chicago: The Swallow Press,
Inc. *Edwin Arlington Robinson*, pp. 341-347. [Reprinted
from 1936 collection.]

AMERICAN LITERATURE: A WORLD VIEW, by Willis Wager. New York:
New York University Press; London: University of London
Press Limited. [*Edwin Arlington Robinson*] pp. 186-189.

AMERICAN POETS: FROM THE PURITANS TO THE PRESENT, by Hyatt H.
Waggoner. Boston: Houghton Mifflin Company. *The Idealist*
in Extremis: *Edwin Arlington Robinson*, pp. 262-292.

AMERICAN LITERARY SCHOLARSHIP: AN ANNUAL / 1966, edited by
James Woodress. Durham, North Carolina: Duke University Press.
Edwin Arlington Robinson, by Gorham Munson, pp. 198-200.

1969

EDWIN ARLINGTON ROBINSON: A CRITICAL STUDY, by Ellsworth
Barnard. New York: Octagon Books. [Originally published, The
Macmillan Company, 1952.]

EDWIN ARLINGTON ROBINSON: CENTENARY ESSAYS, edited by
Ellsworth Barnard. Athens: University of Georgia Press. xx,
192 pp. Contains:

"Of This or That Estate": Robinson's Literary Reputation, by
Ellsworth Barnard, pp. 1-14.

The Strategy of "Flammonde," by William J. Free, pp. 15-30.
"The Man Against the Sky" and the Problem of Faith, by David H.
    Hirsch, pp. 31-42.
The Book of Scattered Lives, by Scott Donaldson, pp. 43-53.
The Metrical Style of E. A. Robinson, by Robert D. Stevick, pp. 54-67.
The Young Robinson as Critic and Self-Critic, by Wallace L.
    Anderson, pp. 68-87.
Robinson's Road to Camelot, by Charles T. Davis, pp. 88-105.
The Transformation of Merlin, by Nathan Comfort Starr,
    pp. 106-119.
Imagery and Theme in "Lancelot," by Christopher Brookhouse,
    pp. 120-129.
A Crisis of Achievement: Robinson's Late Narratives, by Jay Martin,
    pp. 130-156.
Robinson's Modernity, by J. C. Levenson, pp. 157-174. [From
    Virginia Quarterly Review, Vol. XLIV, pp. 590-610, Autumn
    1968.]
Tilbury Town Today, by Radcliffe Squires, pp. 175-183.

FIFTEEN MODERN AMERICAN AUTHORS: A SURVEY OF RESEARCH
    AND CRITICISM, edited by Jackson R. Bryer. Durham, North
    Carolina: Duke University Press. *Edwin Arlington Robinson,*
    by Ellsworth Barnard, pp. 345-367.

APPRECIATION OF EDWIN ARLINGTON ROBINSON: 28 INTERPRETIVE
    ESSAYS, edited by Richard Cary. Waterville, Maine: Colby College
    Press. xiiv, 356 pp. Contains:
On Rereading Robinson, by Archibald MacLeish, pp. 3-5. [From
    Colby Library Quarterly, Series VIII, pp. 217-219, March 1969.]
The Arthur of Edwin Arlington Robinson, by E. Edith Pipkin,
    pp. 6-16. [From *English Journal,* Vol. XIX, pp. 183-195, March
    1930.]
Tilbury Town and Camelot, by Edna Davis Romig, pp. 17-37.
    [From *University of Colorado Studies,* Vol. XIX, pp. 303-326,
    June 1932.]
Robinson as Man and Poet, by Harriet Monroe, pp. 38-42. [From
    Poetry, Vol. XLVI, pp. 150-157, June 1935.]

E. A. Robinson's Later Poems, by David Brown, pp. 34-54. [From
   New England Quarterly, Vol. X, pp. 487-502, September 1937.]
The Optimism Behind Robinson's Tragedies, by Floyd Stovall,
   pp. 55-74. [From *American Literature,* Vol. X, pp. 1-23, March
   1938.]
Tristram the Transcendent, by Frederic Ives Carpenter, pp. 75-90.
   [From *New England Quarterly,* Vol. XI, pp. 501-523,
   September 1938.]
E. A. Robinson and the Cosmic Chill, by Hyatt Howe Waggoner,
   pp. 91-104. [From *New England Quarterly,* Vol. XIII,
   pp. 65-84, March 1940.]
The Shorter Poems of E. A. Robinson, by John R. Doyle, pp. 105-116.
   [From *Bulletin of the Citadel,* Vol. VI, pp. 3-18, 1942.]
The Pernicious Rib: E. A. Robinson's Concept of Feminine Character,
   by Louise Dauner, pp. 117-133 [From *American Literature,*
   Vol. XV, pp. 139-158, May 1943.]
Religious and Social Ideas in the Didactic Work of E. A. Robinson,
   by Yvor Winters, pp. 134-146. [From *Arizona Quarterly,*
   Vol. I, pp. 70-85, Spring 1945.]
"Here Are the Men . . .": E. A. Robinson's Male Character Types, by
   Richard Crowder, pp. 147-163. [From *New England Quarterly,*
   Vol. XVIII, pp. 346-367, September 1945.]
E. A. Robinson: The Lost Tradition, by Louis O. Coxe, pp. 164-177.
   [From *Sewanee Review,* Vol. LXII, pp. 247-266, Spring
   1954.]
Does It Matter How Annandale Went Out?, by David S. Nivison,
   pp. 178-190. [From *Colby Library Quarterly,* Series V,
   pp. 170-185, December 1960.]
Image Patterns in the Poetry of Edwin Arlington Robinson, by
   Charles T. Davis, pp. 191-199. [From *College English,* Vol.
   XXII, pp. 380-386, March 1961.]
E. A. Robinson as Soothsayer, by Richard Cary, pp. 200-209. [From
   Colby Library Quarterly, Series VI, pp. 233-245, June 1963.]
E. A. Robinson's System of Opposites, by James G. Hepburn,
   pp. 210-224. [From *PMLA,* Vol. LXXX, pp. 266-274, June
   1965.]

E. A. Robinson's Poetics, by Lewis E. Weeks, Jr., pp. 225-242. [From
Twentieth Century Literature, Vol. XI, pp. 131-145, October
1965.]

Robinson's "For a Dead Lady": An Exercise in Evaluation, by Clyde
L. Grimm, pp. 243-252. [From *Colby Library Quarterly*, Series
VII, pp. 535-547, December 1967.]

Robinson's Impulse for Narrative, by J. Vail Foy, pp. 253-262. [From
Colby Library Quarterly, Series VIII, pp. 238-249, March
1969.]

Robinson's Use of the Bible, by Nicholas Ayo, pp. 263-275. [From
Colby Library Quarterly, Series VIII, pp. 250-264, March 1969.]

E. A. Robinson's Idea of God, by David H. Burton, pp. 276-288.
[From *Colby Library Quarterly*, Series VIII, pp. 280-294,
June 1969.]

Formulation of E. A. Robinson's Principles of Poetry, by Robert D.
Stevick, pp. 289-300. [From *Colby Library Quarterly*, Series
VIII, pp. 295-308, June 1969.]

The Plays of Edwin Arlington Robinson, by Irving D. Suss,
pp. 301-314. [From *Colby Library Quarterly*, Series VIII,
pp. 347-363, September 1969.]

The Octaves of E. A. Robinson, by Ronald Moran, pp. 315-321.
[From *Colby Library Quarterly*, Series VIII, pp. 363-370,
September 1969.]

E. A. Robinson's Yankee Conscience, by W. R. Robinson,
pp. 322-334. [From *Colby Library Quarterly*, Series VIII,
pp. 371-385, September 1969.]

*He Shouts to See Them Scamper So: E. A. Robinson and the French
Forms*, by Peter Dechert, pp. 335-345. [From *Colby Library
Quarterly*, Series VIII, pp. 386-398, September 1969.]

"The World Is . . . a Kind of Spiritual Kindergarten," by Paul H.
Morrill, pp. 346-356. [From *Colby Library Quarterly*, Series
VIII, pp. 435-448, December 1969.]

EDWIN ARLINGTON ROBINSON: THE LIFE OF POETRY, by Louis O.
Coxe. New York: Pegasus. 188 pp.

A LIBRARY OF LITERARY CRITICISM: MODERN AMERICAN LITERATURE,
compiled and edited by Dorothy Nyren Curley, Maurice Kramer,

and Elaine Fialka Kramer. Fourth enlarged edition. New York:
Frederick Unger Publishing Co. *Robinson, Edwin Arlington
(1869-1935)*, Vol. III, pp. 79-86. [Excerpts from 23 critics.]

THE THIRD BOOK OF CRITICISM, by Randall Jarrell. New York: Farrar,
Straus & Giroux. In article entitled *Fifty Years of American
Poetry*, pp. 296-297. [From *Prairie Schooner*, Spring 1963.]

THE POETRY OF EDWIN ARLINGTON ROBINSON, by Lloyd Morris.
New York: Haskell House; Freeport, New York: Books for Libs.,
Inc.; also Port Washington, New York: Kennikat Press.
[Originally published, George H. Doran Company, 1922.]

DUKEDOM LARGE ENOUGH, by David A. Randall. New York:
Random House. xiv, 368 pp. *Edwin Arlington Robinson*,
pp. 230-234.

AMERICAN LITERARY SCHOLARSHIP: AN ANNUAL / 1967, edited by
James Woodress. Durham, North Carolina: Duke University Press.
E. A. Robinson, by Brom Weber and James Woodress, pp.
221-224.

1970

ARTICLES ON AMERICAN LITERATURE 1950–1967, compiled by Lewis
Leary, with the assistance of Carolyn Bartholet and Catherine
Roth. Durham, North Carolina: Duke University Press. *Robinson,
Edwin Arlington*, pp. 467-470.

ESSAYS IN HONOR OF ESMOND LINWORTH MARILLA, edited by Thomas
Austin Kirby and William John Olive. Baton Rouge: Louisiana
State University Press. *Lorraine and the Sirens: Courtesans in
Two Poems by E. A. Robinson*, by Ronald Moran.

MODERN AMERICAN POETRY: ESSAYS IN CRITICISM, edited by Jerome
Mazzaro. New York: David McKay Company, Inc. *E. A. Robinson
and the Integration of Self*, by H. R. Wolf, pp. 40-59.

EDWIN ARLINGTON ROBINSON: A COLLECTION OF CRITICAL ESSAYS,
edited by Francis Murphy. Twentieth Century Views. Englewood
Cliffs, New Jersey: Prentice-Hall, Inc. vi, 186 pp. Contains:
Introduction, by Francis Murphy, pp. 1-7.

A Cool Master, by Yvor Winters, pp. 8-15. [From *Poetry*, Vol. XIX, pp. 277-288, February 1922.]

Three Reviews, by Conrad Aiken, pp. 15-28. [From *A Reviewer's ABC* (New York: Meridan Books, Inc., 1958), pp. 333-346.]

Robinson in America, by Morton Dauwen Zabel, pp. 29-32. [From *Poetry*, Vol. XLVI, pp. 157-162, June 1935.]

Introduction to "King Jasper," by Robert Frost, pp. 33-39. [From *King Jasper*, by Edwin Arlington Robinson (New York: The Macmillan Company, 1953), pp. v-xv.]

The Shorter Poems, by Yvor Winters, pp. 40-59. [From *Edwin Arlington Robinson* (New York: New Directions, 1946), pp. 29-60.]

E. A. Robinson: The Lost Tradition, by Louis O. Coxe, pp. 60-76. [From *Sewanee Review*, Vol. LXII, pp. 247-266, Spring 1954.]

Edwin Arlington Robinson: The Many Truths, by James Dickey, pp. 77-94. [From *Selected Poems of Edwin Arlington Robinson*, edited by Morton Dauwen Zabel (New York: The Macmillan Company, 1965), pp. xi-xxviii.]

One Kind of Traditional Poet, by Edwin S. Fussell, pp. 95-109. [From *Edwin Arlington Robinson: The Literary Background of a Traditional Poet* (Berkeley: University of California Press, 1954), pp. 171-186.]

Robinson's Inner Fire, by Josephine Miles, pp. 110-116.

The "New" Poetry: Robinson and Frost, by Warner Berthoff, pp. 117-127. [From *The Ferment of Realism: American Literature, 1884-1919* (New York: The Free Press, 1965), pp. 263-277.]

The Alienated Self, by W. R. Robinson, pp. 128-147. [From *Edwin Arlington Robinson: A Poetry of the Act* (Cleveland: The Press of Western Reserve University, 1967), pp. 75-95.]

E. A. Robinson: The Cosmic Chill, by Hyatt H. Waggoner, pp. 148-163, [From *The Heel of Elohim* (Norman: The University of Oklahoma Press, 1950), pp. 18-40,]

Robinson's Modernity, by J. C. Levenson, pp. 164-181. [From *Virgina Quarterly Review*, Vol. XLIV, pp. 590-610, Autumn 1968.]

BIBLIOGRAPHY OF BIBLIOGRAPHIES IN AMERICAN LITERATURE, by
Charles H. Nilon. New York and London: R. R. Bowker Company.
Robinson, Edwin Arlington, pp. 235-237.
EDWIN ARLINGTON ROBINSON: A BIO-BIBLIOGRAPHY [by John William
Pye]. Hartford, Connecticut: Watkinson Library, Trinity College.
viii, 48 pp.
AMERICAN LITERARY SCHOLARSHIP: AN ANNUAL / 1968, edited by
J. Albert Robbins. Durham, North Carolina: Duke University Press.
Robinson Jeffers, E. A. Robinson, E. E. Cummings,
by Gorham Munson and Ann Stanford, pp. 238-240.

B. Periodicals

1894

In an article entitled WRECK OF THE MAYFLOWER, by W[illiam] H[enry] Thorne. *The Globe* (New York), Vol. IV, p. 801, September.

1904

A POET IN THE SURWAY [by Joseph Lewis French]. *The World* (New York), May 15, The World Magazine, p. 10.
[AN APPRECIATION] by Edmund Clarence Stedman. *Ibid.*

1905

In article entitled TOPICS UPPERMOST. *The New York Times Saturday Review of Books* (New York), August 19, p. 537.
THE PRESIDENT AS A CRITIC OF POETRY. *Current Literature* (New York), Vol. XXXIX, pp. 388-389, October.

1912

A DISCUSSION OF THE EXACT VALUE OF ROBINSON'S POETRY, by Louis V[ernon] Ledoux. *The New York Times Review of Books* (New York), September 29, p. 533.
EDWIN ARLINGTON ROBINSON. *The Sunday Journal* (Minneapolis), November 3, Woman's Section, p. 5.
EDWIN ARLINGTON ROBINSON, by Hermann Hagedorn. *The New York Times Review of Books* (New York), December 1, p. 747.

1919

A POET'S BIRTHDAY. *The New York Times* (New York), December 21, Section III, p. 1. [Reprinted, *Literary Digest*, 1920.]

1920

In article entitled Maine's Contribution to Literature, by John
Clair Minot. *Maine Library Bulletin* (Augusta), Vol. IX,
pp. 58-59, January.

A Poet's Birthday. *The Literary Digest* (New York), Vol. LXIV,
pp. 32-33, January 10.

1921

Insight and Epithet, by W. W. *John O'London's Weekly* (London),
Vol. VI, pp. 364-365, December 17.

Mr. Edwin Arlington Robinson Abroad, by John Gould Fletcher.
The Living Age (Boston), Vol. CCCXI, p. 744, December 17.

1922

An American Bard and the British Reviewers. *The Living Age*
(Boston), Vol. CCCXV, p. 244, October 28.

Author's Club Hails Poet: E. A. Robinson's Poems Voted Most
Notable 1921 American Publication. *The New York Times*
(New York), January 27, Section I, p. 13.

Yale Bestows Academic Honors. *The New York Times* (New
York). June 22, Section I, p. 6.

1923

In article entitled Nationalism and Imagism in Modern American
Poetry, by Richard Foster Jones, *Washington University Studies*
(St. Louis, Missouri), Vol. XI, pp. 97-130, October.

1925

Edwin Arlington Robinson's Treatment of the Arthurian
Legend, by Charles Cestre. *The Bryn Mawr Alumnae Bulletin*
(Philadelphia), Vol. V, November, pp. 5-15 [Reprinted in his
An Introduction to Edwin Arlington Robinson, 1930, pp. 67-118.]

1927

ROBINSON. *The Literary Digest* (New York), Vol. XCIII, p. 28, May 28. [See also p. 33.]

1928

WINS PULITZER PRIZE: TRISTRAM. *The New York Times* (New York), May 8, Section I, p. 4.

EDITORIAL STAFF. *The Book League Monthly* (New York), Vol. I, p. 1, November.

1929

OUR EDITORS: A SERIES OF STUDIES: EDWIN ARLINGTON ROBINSON, by Mark Van Doren. *The Book League Monthly* (New York), Vol. I, pp. 271-273, January.

CAVENDER'S HOUSE. *The Book League Monthly* (New York), Vol. II, p. [I], May.

CAVENDER'S HOUSE. *The Book League Monthly* (New York), Vol. II, p. 187, June.

LAZARUS IN MODERN LITERATURE, by Levette J. Davidson. *The English Journal* (Chicago), Vol. XVIII, pp. 462-463, June.

E. A. ROBINSON GETS MEDAL FOR POETRY. *The New York Times* (New York), November 15, Section I, p. 32.

ROBINSON, POET, 60 YEARS OLD. *The New York Times* (New York), December 23, Section I, p. 9.

1930

IN MEMORIAM TWENTY YEARS AFTER: OCTOBER, 1910, TO OCTOBER, 1920: A SONNET TO EDWIN ARLINGTON ROBINSON, by Percy MacKaye. *Harvard Graduates' Magazine* (Cambridge) Vol. XXXIX, p. 140, December. [Also in *The Boston Evening Transcript* (Boston), October 18, 1930, Section I, p. 9.]

1932

In article entitled THE NEW AGE OF AMERICAN POETRY, by John Macy. *Current History* (New York), Vol. XXXV, pp. 554-555, January.

EINSTEIN IS TERSE IN RULE FOR SUCCESS: FIVE NOTABLES GIVE
ADVICE: EDWIN ARLINGTON ROBINSON. *The New York Times*
(New York), June 20, Section I, p. 17.

In article entitled THE POETRY REVIVAL OF 1914, by Edgar Lee Masters.
The American Mercury (New York), Vol. XXVI, pp. 274-275,
July.

1933

EDWIN ARLINGTON ROBINSON'S THREE POEMS, by Robert C[hapman]
Bates. *The Yale University Library Gazette* (New Haven),
Vol. VIII, pp. 81-82, October.

1935

[ON ROBINSON'S ILLNESS, DEATH, AND WILL]. *The New York Times*
(New York), April 4, Section I, p. 215; April 5, Section I, p. 19;
April 6, Section I, p. 15; April 7, Section I, p. 40; April 8, Section
I, pp. 18, 19; April 9, Section I, p. 19; April 20, Section I, pp. 11,
26; August 31, Section I, p. 13.

EDWIN ROBINSON DIES AS FRIENDS SIT AT BEDSIDE. *New York World
Telegram* (New York), April 6, Section I, p. 14.

E. A. ROBINSON, PULITZER PRIZE POET, DIES HERE. *New York
Herald-Tribune* (New York), April 6, Section I, p. 19.

AMERICA'S CHIEF POET, by E[dward] B[olland] Osborn. *The Morning
Post* (London), April 8, p. 6.

SONNETS (ON THE DEATH OF EDWIN ARLINGTON ROBINSON)
[verse], by "Jessup." *Chicago Daily Tribune* (Chicago), April 13,
p. 12.

OBITUARIES: EDWIN ARLINGTON ROBINSON. *The Publishers' Weekly*
(New York), Vol. CXXVII, p. 1520, April 13.

In article entitled THE PHEONIX NEST, by William Rose Benét. *The
Saturday Review of Literature* (New York), Vol. XI, p. 628, April
13.

DIED [EDWIN ARLINGTON ROBINSON]. *Time* (New York), Vol. XXV,
p. 72, April 15.

THE EXCELLENT CAREER. *The Commonweal* (New York), Vol. XXI, p. 694, April 19. [See also pp. 708-709.]

TWO SONNETS, by Carl J. Weber. *The Saturday Review of Literature* (New York), Vol. XI, p. 648, April 27.

E. A. ROBINSON AND HARDY, by Carl J. Weber. *The Nation* (New York), Vol. CXL, p. 508. May 1. [Also in *The Saturday Review of Literature* (New York), Vol. XI, p. 648, April 27.]

EDWIN ARLINGTON ROBINSON. *Modern Literature* (Columbus, Ohio), Vol. III, p. 9, May 1-14.

EDWIN ARLINGTON ROBINSON. *Modern Literature* (Columbus, Ohio), Vol. IV, p. 12, September 15-30.

EDWIN ARLINGTON ROBINSON: LOOKING BACK ON OUR FIRST CONTEMPORARY POET, by Dorothy Emerson. *Scholastic* (Chicago), Vol. XXVII, pp. 9-10, October 12.

ROBINSON AND FROST, by V. Foster Hopper. *The Saturday Review of Literature* (New York), Vol. XIII, p. 9, November 2. [Reply to Louis V. Ledoux, *ibid.*, Vol. XII, pp. 3-4, 16, 18, October 19.]

[ON ROBINSON MEMORIAL]. *Poetry* (Chicago), Vol. XLVI, p. 293, August; Vol. XLVII, p. 172, December.

1936

EDWIN ARLINGTON ROBINSON, by Georges Roth. *Larousse Mensuel Illustré* (Paris), Vol. X, pp. 339-340, February.

EDWIN ARLINGTON ROBINSON. *The Library Journal* (New York), Vol. LXI, p. 158, February 15.

ROBINSON MEMORIAL. *The Publishers' Weekly* (New York), Vol. CXXIX, p. 895, February 22.

A BOOK AND ITS AUTHOR, by Laura E[lizabeth] Richards. *Yankee* (Dublin, New Hampshire), Vol. II, pp. 26-29, June.

[TRIBUTE TO ROBINSON] by William Lyon Phelps. *New York Herald Tribune* (New York), November 13, pp. 14-15. [Reprinted in his *Autobiography with Letters*, 1939, pp. 693-698 and in *Commemorative Tributes, The American Academy of Arts and Letters*, New York, Academy Publication No. 95, 1939, pp. 9-19.]

1937

EDWIN ARLINGTON ROBINSON [verse], by Allen E[arl] Woodall.
Poet Lore (Boston), Vol. XLIII, No. 4, p. 363.

EARLY LETTERS OF EDWIN ARLINGTON ROBINSON: FIRST SERIES, by
Daniel Gregory Mason. *The Virginia Quarterly Review*
(Charlottesville, Virginia), Vol. XIII, pp. 52-69, Winter.

EDWIN ARLINGTON ROBINSON TO DANIEL GREGORY MASON:
SECOND SERIES, by Daniel Gregory Mason. *The Virginia Quarterly
Review* (Charlottesville, Virginia), Vol. XIII, pp. 223-240,
Spring.

In article entitled THE PHOENIX NEST, by William Rose Benét. *The
Saturday Review of Literature* (New York), Vol. XVI, p. 19,
May 22. [Contains a letter from Howard G. Schmitt regarding
textual changes in *Amaranth*.]

"THE UNACCREDITED PROFESSION," by Winfield Townley Scott.
Poetry (Chicago), Vol. L, pp. 150-154, June.

EDWIN ARLINGTON ROBINSON, HIMSELF, by Florence Peltier. *The
Mark Twain Quarterly* (Webster Groves, Missouri), Vol. I, pp. 6,
11-14, Summer.

E. A. ROBINSON'S LATER POEMS, by David Brown. *The New England
Quarterly* (Norwood, Massachusetts), Vol. X, pp. 487-502,
September. [Reprinted in Richard Cary, *Appreciation* . . . See 1969
above.]

PORTRAIT OF EDWIN ARLINGTON ROBINSON [verse], by John Gould
Fletcher. *The North American Review* (Concord, New Hampshire),
Vol. CCXLIV, pp. 24-26, Autumn.

A NOTE ON *AVON'S HARVEST*, by David Brown. *American
Literature* (Durham, North Carolina), Vol. IX, pp. 343-349,
November.

1938

THE POET AT THE DINNER TABLE, by Olivia H[oward] D[unbar]
Torrence. *The Colophon* (New York), N. S., Vol. III, pp.
93-99, Winter.

THE OPTIMISM BEHIND ROBINSON'S TRAGEDIES, by Floyd Stovall. *American Literature* (Durham, North Carolina), Vol. X, pp. 1-23, March. [Reprinted in Richard Cary, *Appreciation* . . . See 1969 above.]

E. A. ROBINSON: 1869-1935 [by Cyril Clemens]. *The Mark Twain Quarterly* (Webster Groves, Missouri), Vol. II, pp. 1-2, Spring.

THE BIG BED, by John Cowper Powys. *Ibid.*, p. 2.

EDWIN ARLINGTON ROBINSON . . . MAKER OF MYTHS, by Charles Cestre. *Ibid.*, pp. 3-8, 24.

ROBINSON AS I SAW HIM, by Richard Burton. *Ibid.*, p. 9.

IN MEMORIAM: WRITTEN IN 1935, by Louis V[ernon] Ledoux, *Ibid.*, p. 10. (Originally published in *The Saturday Review of Literature* [New York], Vol. XI, p. 621, April 13, 1935.)

PERFECT ARTISTIC INTEGRITY, by William Rose Benét. *Ibid.*, p. 10.

[AN APPRECIATION] by John G[neisenau] Neihardt. *Ibid.*, p. 10.

THE COSMIC HUMORIST, by Arthur E[dwin] DuBois. *Ibid.*, pp. 11-13, 24.

A LETTER FROM ROLLO WALTER BROWN, by Rollo Walter Brown. *Ibid.*, pp. 14, 24.

ROBINSON'S INTEREST IN MUSIC, by Mabel Daniels. *Ibid.*, pp. 15, 24. [Originally published in *Portland Sunday Telegram* (Portland, Maine), April 21, 1935, Section A, p. 7.]

ROBINSON AT THE MACDOWELL COLONY, by Mrs. Edward MacDowell. *Ibid.*, p. 16.

FROM THE OFFICIAL BIOGRAPHER, by Hermann Hagedorn. *Ibid.*, p. 16.

[AN APPRECIATION] by C[harles] T[ownsend] Copeland. *Ibid.*, p. 16.

DEAN OF AMERICAN POETS PAYS TRIBUTE, by Edwin Markham. *Ibid.*, p. 17.

ROBINSON COLLECTION AT GARDINER, MAINE, by Cyril Clemens. *Ibid.*, p. 18.

ROBINSON AT HARVARD, by G[eorge] W[arrington] Latham. *Ibid.*, pp. 19-20.

A FRIEND OF YOUNG POETS, by John Hall Wheelock. *Ibid.*, p. 20.

[AN APPRECIATION] by Christopher Morley. *Ibid.*, p. 20.

THE LAST LOOK [verse], by Mark Van Doren. *Ibid.*, p. 21.

EPITAPH ON A POET [verse], by Arthur Guiterman. *Ibid.*, p. 12.

64

EDWIN ARLINGTON ROBINSON, by Dorothy Ulrich. *Avocations* (New York), Vol. II, pp. 248-253, June. (Reprinted as a pamphlet, 1940.)
EDWARD [*sic*] ARLINGTON ROBINSON, by Thomas J. Brosnan. *Connecticut Teacher* (Hartford), Vol. V, pp. 3-4, 6, June.
A POET AT THE PHONIC SHRINE, by Charles Beecher Hogan. *The Colophon* (New York), N. S., Vol. III, pp. 359-363, Summer.
TRISTRAM THE TRANSCENDENT, by Frederic Ives Carpenter. *The New England Quarterly* (Orono, Maine), Vol. XI, pp. 501-523, September. [Reprinted in Richard Cary, *Appreciation* . . . See 1969, above.]
LIBRARY NOTES FOR E. A. R.'s BIRTHDAY [by Carl Jefferson Weber]. *The Colby Mercury* (Waterville, Maine), Vol. VI, pp. 205-213, November.
"THE SOUND OF CORNISH WAVES COLD UPON CORNISH ROCKS," by Carl J[efferson] Weber. *Ibid.*, pp. 215-216.

1939

EDWIN ARLINGTON ROBINSON, by William Lyon Phelps. *Commemorative Tributes, The American Academy of Arts and Letters* (New York), Academy Publication No. 95, pp. 9-19. (Originally published in *New York Herald Tribune* [New York], November 13, 1936, pp. 14-15, and in Mr. Phelps's *Autobiography with Letters*, 1939, pp. 693-698.)
THE FIRST EDITION OF E. A. ROBINSON'S THE PETERBOROUGH IDEA, by Leonidas Warren Payne, Jr. *The University of Texas Studies in English* (Austin), July 8, pp. 219-231.
ROBINSONIANA, by C[arl] Lennart Carlson. *The Colby Mercury* (Waterville, Maine), Vol. VI, pp. 281-284, December.
A BIOGRAPHER OF SOULS, by Bruce Swift. *The Christian Leader* (Boston), Vol. CXXI, pp. 1194-1195, December 16.

1940

E. A. ROBINSON AND THE COSMIC CHILL, by Hyatt Howe Waggoner. *The New England Quarterly* (Orono, Maine), Vol. XIII, pp. 65-84, March. [Reprinted, revised, in his *The Heel of Elohim*, 1950,

pp. 18-40. Reprinted in Richard Cary, *Appreciation* . . . See
1969, above.]
GARDINER ASSOCIATIONS OF POET RECALLED BY PRESENT RESIDENT,
by Alice Frost Lord. *Lewiston Journal Illustrated Magazine Section*
(Lewiston, Maine), March 30, p. 8.
GARDINER WOMAN CHERISHES LETTERS FROM POET, ROBINSON, by
Alice Frost Lord. *Lewiston Journal Illustrated Magazine
Section* (Lewiston, Maine), April 13, p. 8.
THE PSYCHOLOGY OF ROBINSON, by Sister Mary Catherine. *The Catholic
Educational Review* (Washington, D. C.), Vol. XXXVIII,
pp. 354-360, June.
A MAINE POET IN A MAINE COLLEGE, by Carl J[efferson] Weber.
The Colby Alumnus (Waterville, Maine), Vol. XXX, pp. 10-12,
November.

1941

MEMORIES OF EDWIN ARLINGTON ROBINSON, by Mowry Saben.
The Colby Mercury (Waterville, Maine), Vol. VII, pp. 13-14,
January.
CAPTAIN CRAIG, by C. Elta Van Norman. *College English* (Champaign,
Illinois), Vol. II, pp. 462-475, February.
EDWIN ARLINGTON ROBINSON, by Jessie B[elle] Rittenhouse. *Rollins
College Bulletin* (Winter Park, Florida), Vol. XXXVI, pp. 5-10,
June. [Selected Faculty Papers.]
POETRY ALBUM: EDWIN ARLINGTON ROBINSON. *Scholastic* (New
York), Vol. XXXIX, p. 22, October 13.
THREE NEWLY FOUND ARTICLES BY EDWIN ARLINGTON ROBINSON,
by Carl J. Weber. *The Colby Mercury* (Waterville, Maine),
Vol. VII, pp. 69-72, December.

1942

THE SHORTER POEMS OF E. A. ROBINSON, by John R. Doyle. *Bulletin
of the Citadel* (Charleston, South Carolina), Vol. VI, pp. 3-18.
[Reprinted in Richard Cary, *Appreciation* . . . See 1969, above.]

Edwin Arlington Robinson — New England Poet-Philosopher,
by Thomas Wearing. *Colgate-Rochester Divinity School Bulletin*
(Hamilton and Rochester, New York), Vol. XIV, pp.
162-174, February.

Avon and Cavender: Two Children of the Night, by Louise
Dauner. *American Literature* (Durham, North Carolina),
Vol. XIV, pp. 55-65, March.

Robinson's Letters to George Burnham, by James M. L. Bates.
The Colby Mercury (Waterville, Maine), Vol. VII, pp. 93-94,
May.

Additions to Our Robinson Collection [by Carl J. Weber]. *The
Colby Mercury* (Waterville, Maine), Vol. VII, pp. 94-96, May.

A Robinson Wild-Goose Chase [by Carl J. Weber]. *The Colby
Mercury* (Waterville, Maine), Vol. VII, p. 96, May.

In article entitled News from the Rare Book Sellers, by Jacob
Blanck. *The Publishers' Weekly* (New York), Vol. CXLI, p. 1923,
May 23.

Edwin Arlington Robinson in the Hands of the Reviewers,
by Winifred Burns, *Poet-Lore* (Boston), Vol. XLVIII, pp. 164-175,
Summer.

Some Recollections of E. A. Robinson, by William Thomas Walsh.
The Catholic World (New York), Vol. CLV, pp. 522-531,
703-712, August, September.

Vox Clamantis: Edwin Arlington Robinson as a Critic of
American Democracy, by Louise Dauner. *The New England
Quarterly* (Brunswick, Maine), Vol. XV, pp. 401-426, September.

The Robinson Gift, by R. C. Bates. *The Yale University Library
Gazette* (New Haven), Vol. XVII, pp. 33-35, October.

Edwin Arlington Robinson, Journalist, by Alice Meacham
Williams. *The New England Quarterly* (Brunswick, Maine),
Vol. XV, pp. 715-724, December.

1943

Some Robinson Letters in My Collection, by Howard George
Schmitt. *Colby Library Quarterly* (Waterville, Maine), Series I,
pp. 8-12, January.

ROBINSON AND PRAED, by Hoyt H. Hudson. *Poetry* (Chicago),
Vol. LXI, pp. 612-620, February.
[THE MEANING OF "THE WHIP," by Ben Ray Redman] in article
entitled THE PHOENIX NEST, by William Rose Benét. *The Saturday
Review of Literature* (New York), Vol. XXVI, p. 18,
February 20.
ROBINSON AND THE WAR, by H. B. Collamore. *Colby Library
Quarterly* (Waterville, Maine), Series I, pp. 30-31, March.
ROBINSON'S PROSE: A RETRACTION, by Carl J. Weber. *Colby Library
Quarterly* (Waterville, Maine), Series 1, pp. 31-32, March.
ROBINSON'S "THE WHIP," by Henry Pettit. *The Explicator*
(Fredericksburg, Virginia), Vol. I, Item 50, April.
E. A. ROBINSON, in article entitled THE PHOENIX NEST, by William
Rose Benét. *The Saturday Review of Literature* (New York),
Vol. XXVI, p. 54, April 17. [On "The Whip."]
THE PERNICIOUS RIB: E. A. ROBINSON'S CONCEPT OF FEMININE
CHARACTER, by Louise Dauner. *American Literature* (Durham,
North Carolina), Vol. XV, pp. 139-158, May. [Reprinted in
Richard Cary, *Appreciation* . . . See 1969, above.]
A POET FOR PASTORS, by Samuel G. Beers, *Religion in Life* (New
York), Vol. XII, pp. 421-430, Summer.
THE ORIGINAL OF ROBINSON'S "CAPTAIN CRAIG," by W. Denham
Sutcliffe. *The New England Quarterly* (Brunswick, Maine),
Vol. XVI, pp. 407-431, September.
POET AND PRESIDENT, by Carl J. Weber. *The New England Quarterly*
(Brunswick, Maine), Vol. XVI, pp. 615-626, December.

1944

STUDIES IN EDWIN ARLINGTON ROBINSON, by Louise Dauner. *University
of Iowa Programs Announcing Candidates for Higher Degrees*
(Iowa City).
SOPHOCLES AND "CAPTAIN CRAIG," by James A. Notopoulos.
The New England Quarterly (Brunswick, Maine),
Vol. XVII, p. 109, March.

THE VEIN OF COMEDY IN E. A. ROBINSON'S POETRY, by Horace
Gregory and Marya Zaturenska. *The American Bookman*
(New York), Vol. I, pp. 43-64, Fall.

READING AND MEDITATING: EDWIN ARLINGTON ROBINSON'S POEMS
[verse], by James Norman Hall, *The Atlantic Monthly* (Boston),
Vol. CLXXIV, pp. 57-58, September.

EDWIN ARLINGTON ROBINSON AS I KNEW HIM, by Fredericka Beatty.
The South Atlantic Quarterly (Durham, North Carolina),
Vol. XLIII, pp. 375-381, October.

ROBINSON'S "LUKE HAVERGAL," by Walter Gierasch. *The
Explicator* (Fredericksburg, Virginia), Vol. III, Item 8, October.
[Abridged in *The Case for Poetry*, edited by Frederick L. Gwynn,
Ralph W. Condee, and Arthur O. Lewis, Jr. (Englewood Cliffs,
New Jersey: Prentice-Hall, Inc., 1954), p. 297.]

ROBINSON'S "LUKE HAVERGAL," by A. A. Raven. *The Explicator*
(Fredericksburg, Virginia), Vol. III, Item 24, December.

E. A. ROBINSON'S TRANSLATION OF SOPHOCLES, by Carl J. Weber.
The New England Quarterly (Brunswick, Maine), Vol. XVII,
pp. 604-605, December.

1945

RELIGIOUS AND SOCIAL IDEAS IN THE DIDACTIC WORK OF E. A.
ROBINSON, by Yvor Winters. *The Arizona Quarterly* (Tucson),
Vol. I, pp. 70-85, Spring. [Reprinted in Richard Cary,
Appreciation . . . See 1969, above.]

SOME ASPECTS OF THE PHILOSOPHY OF EDWIN ARLINGTON ROBINSON:
SELF-KNOWLEDGE, SELF-ACCEPTANCE, AND CONSCIENCE, by
Seymour Betsky. *Harvard University Summary of Theses*,
1943-1945 (Cambridge), pp. 457-460.

THREE STUDIES OF E. A. ROBINSON: HIS MALE CHARACTERS, HIS
EMERGENCE, AND HIS CONTEMPORANEOUS REPUTATION, by
Richard Crowder. *University of Iowa Programs Announcing
Candidates for Higher Degrees* (Iowa City).

HE SAW THE GLEAM OF LANCELOT: EDWIN ARLINGTON ROBINSON,
1869-1935, *Senior Scholastic* (New York), Vol. XLVI, p. 17,
April 2.

ROBINSON'S "LUKE HAVERGAL," by Mathilde M. Parlett. *The Explicator* (Fredericksburg, Virginia), Vol. III, Item 57, June.

ROBINSON'S "FOR A DEAD LADY," by R. H. Super. *The Explicator* (Fredericksburg, Virginia), Vol. III, Item 60, June.

"HERE ARE THE MEN . . .": E. A. ROBINSON'S MALE CHARACTER TYPES, by Richard Crowder. *The New England Quarterly* (Brunswick, Maine), Vol. XVIII, pp. 346-367, September. [Reprinted in Richard Cary, *Appreciation* . . . See 1969, above.]

ROBINSON'S "AN OLD STORY," by Richard Crowder. *The Explicator* (Fredericksburg, Virginia), Vol. IV, Item 22, December.

1946

E. A. ROBINSON'S CRAFTSMANSHIP: OPINIONS OF CONTEMPORARY POETS, by Richard Crowder. *Modern Language Notes* (Baltimore), Vol. LXI, pp. 1-14, January.

THE EMERGENCE OF E. A. ROBINSON, by Richard Crowder. *The South Atlantic Quarterly* (Durham, North Carolina), Vol. XLV, pp. 89-98, January.

ROBINSON'S "THE SHEAVES," by Richard Crowder. *The Explicator* (Fredericksburg, Virginia), Vol. IV, Item 38, March.

YOUR TOWN: YOUR PEOPLE ["MR. FLOOD'S PARTY"]. *Scholastic* (New York), Vol. XLVIII, p. 23, May 13.

POETAS Y PROSISTAS AMERICANOS: I. EDWIN ARLINGTON ROBINSON. II. THOMAS WOLFE, by Gastón Figueira. *Revista Iberoamericano* (Iowa City, Iowa), Vol. XI, pp. 329-332, October.

ROBINSON'S "FOR A DEAD LADY," by Richard Crowder. *The Explicator* (Fredericksburg, Virginia), Vol. V., Item 19, December.

1947

SURVIVALS, in article entitled THE PHOENIX NEST, by William Rose Benét. *The Saturday Review of Literature* (New York), Vol. XXX, p. 32, January 18.

THE JUBILEE OF ROBINSON'S TORRENT, by Carl J. Weber. *Colby Library Quarterly* (Waterville, Maine), Series II, pp. 1-12, February.

A New Poem by Edwin Arlington Robinson [by Carl J. Weber]. *Colby Library Quarterly* (Waterville, Maine), Series II, pp. 12-13, February.

[Robinson's "The Whip," in Yvor Winter's Book] in article entitled The Phoenix Nest, by William Rose Benét. *The Saturday Review of Literature* (New York), Vol. XXX, p. 48, March 8.

Robinson's "Sonnet: Oh for a Poet," by M. N. O. *The Explicator* (Fredericksburg, Virginia), Vol. V, Query 21, May.

Robinson's "For a Dead Lady," by R. H. Super. *The Explicator* (Fredericksburg, Virginia), Vol. V, Item 60, June.

E. A. Robinson and A. E. Housman, by William White. *Colby Library Quarterly* (Waterville, Maine), Series II, pp. 42-43, August.

[Additions to the Census of the *TORRENT*]. *Colby Library Quarterly* (Waterville, Maine), Series II, p. 52, August.

E. A. Robinson's Camelot, by Richard Crowder. *College English* (Champaign, Illinois), Vol. IX, pp. 72-79, November.

Robinson's "Veteran Sirens," by Laurence Perrine. *The Explicator* (Lynchburg, Virginia), Vol. VI, Item 13, November.

News for the Rare Book Sellers, by Jacob Blanck. *The Publishers' Weekly* (New York), Vol. CLII, p. B354, November 22.

1948

Edwin Arlington Robinson: A Descriptive List of the Lewis M. Isaacs Collection of Robinsoniana, by Edith J. R. Isaacs. *Bulletin of the New York Public Library* (New York), Vol. LII, pp. 211-233, May.

Robinson's "Tristram," IX-X, by Laurence Perrine. *The Explicator* (Lynchburg, Virginia), Vol. VI, Item 44, May.

With Admiration and Love, by Carl J. Weber. *Colby Library Quarterly* (Waterville, Maine), Series II, pp. 85-108, May.

News Notes. *Poetry* (Chicago), Vol. LXXIV, p. 122, May.

E. A. Robinson: Vision and Voice, by Sister M. B. Quinn. *America* (New York), Vol. LXXIX, pp. 141-143, May 15.

Two More "Torrents," by Carl J. Weber. *Colby Library Quarterly* (Waterville, Maine), Series II, pp. 122-123, August.

ROBINSON'S "LUKE HAVERGAL," by Richard Crowder. *The Explicator* (Lynchburg, Virginia), Vol. VII, Item 15, November.

EDWIN ARLINGTON ROBINSON: DEFEAT AND TRIUMPH, by Malcolm Cowley. *The New Republic* (New York), Vol. CXIX, pp. 26-30, December 6.

1949

TWO FRIENDS OF ROBINSON [by Carl J. Weber]. *Colby Library Quarterly* (Waterville, Maine), Series II, pp. 147-152, February.

ROBINSON'S "TRISTRAM," by Laurence Perrine. *The Explicator* (Lynchburg, Virginia), Vol. VII, Item 33, March.

TWO MORE "TORRENTS" TURN UP [by Carl J. Weber]. *Colby Library Quarterly* (Waterville, Maine), Series II, pp. 161-162, May.

TRYING TO SPELL GOD: A STUDY OF EDWIN ARLINGTON ROBINSON, by Mattie M. Dykes. *Northwest Missouri State Teachers College Studies* (Maryville, Missouri), Vol. XIII, pp. 85-124, June.

MRS. MACDOWELL AND HER COLONY, by R. W. Brown. *The Atlantic Monthly* (Boston), Vol. CLXXX, pp. 42-46, July.

THE LEDOUX COLLECTION OF EDWIN ARLINGTON ROBINSON, by Léonie Adams. *The Library of Congress Quarterly Journal of Current Acquisitions* (Washington), Vol. VII, pp. 9-13, November.

TRADITIONALISM IN AMERICAN POETRY, by Henry Steele Commager. *The Nineteenth Century and After* (London), Vol. CXLVI, pp. 311-326, November.

E. A. ROBINSON'S SYMPHONY: "THE MAN WHO DIED TWICE," by Richard Crowder. *College English* (Champaign, Illinois), Vol. XI, pp. 141-144, December.

E. A. ROBINSON SPEAKS OF MUSIC, by Lewis M. Isaacs. *The New England Quarterly* (Brunswick, Maine), Vol. XXII, pp. 499-510, December.

ROBINSON'S "EROS TURANNOS," by Laurence Perrine. *The Explicator* (Lynchburg, Virginia), Vol. VIII, Item 20, December.

1950

ROBINSON'S "THE FIELD OF GLORY," by Richard Crowder. *The Explicator* (Lynchburg, Virginia), Vol. VIII, Item 31, February.

72

JOURNEY TO HEAD TIDE, by M. C. Jane. *The Christian Science Monitor*, Magazine Section, Vol. XLII, p. 10, February 25.

ROBINSON'S "MR. FLOOD'S PARTY," by E. Sydnor Ownbey. *The Explicator* (Lynchburg, Virginia), Vol. VIII, Item 47, April.

E. A. ROBINSON'S "MR. FLOOD'S PARTY," by Willis D. Jacobs. *College English* (Champaign, Illinois), Vol. XII, p. 110, November.

HUMPHRY'S CATALOGUE OF ROBINSON'S LIBRARY, by Carl J. Weber. *Colby Library Quarterly* (Waterville, Maine), Series II, p. 271-272, November.

1951

AN UNPUBLISHED POEM BY E. A. ROBINSON, by Edwin S. Fussell. *American Literature* (Durham, North Carolina), Vol. XXII, 487-488, January.

ROBINSON'S "FOR A DEAD LADY," by E[dwin] S. Fussell. *The Explicator* (Lynchburg, Virginia), Vol. IX, Item 33, March.

THE SWORD AND THE DRAGON, by Lincoln Fitzell. *The South Atlantic Quarterly* (Durham, North Carolina), Vol. L, pp. 214-232 [229-230]. April. [On "Luke Havergal."]

ROBINSON TO MOODY: TEN UNPUBLISHED LETTERS, by Edwin S. Fussell. *American Literature* (Durham, North Carolina), Vol. XXIII, pp. 173-187, May.

A NOTE ON E. A. ROBINSON'S "CREDO," by Edwin S. Fussell. *Modern Language Notes* (Baltimore), Vol. LXVI, pp. 398-400, June.

1952

ROBINSON'S "NEW ENGLAND," by Richard E. Amacher. *The Explicator* (Lynchburg, Virginia), Vol. X, Item 33, March.

ROBINSON'S "NEW ENGLAND," by H. H. Waggoner. *The Explicator* (Lynchburg, Virginia), Vol. X, Item 33, March.

ROBINSON'S "FOR A DEAD LADY," by Sylvia Hart and Estelle Paige [not W. H. French, listed in error]. *The Explicator* (Lynchburg, Virginia), Vol. X, Item 51, May.

1953

"MAN AGAINST THE SKY," by Richard Crowder. *College English* (Champaign, Illinois), Vol. XIV, pp. 269-276, February.
ROBINSON'S "LOST ANCHORS," by Celeste Turner Wright. *The Explicator* (Lynchburg, Virginia), Vol. XI, Item 57, June.

1954

ANOTHER "TORRENT" TURNS UP [by Carl J. Weber]. *Colby Library Quarterly* (Waterville, Maine), Series III, p. 220, February.
E. A. ROBINSON: THE LOST TRADITION, by Louis O. Coxe. *The Sewanee Review* (Sewanee, Tennessee), Vol. LXII, pp. 247-266, Spring. [Reprinted in Richard Cary, *Appreciation* . . . See 1969, above; and in Francis Murphy, *A Collection* . . . See 1970, above.]
TWO LETTERS OF EDWIN ARLINGTON ROBINSON: A NOTE ON HIS EARLY CRITICAL RECEPTION, by Robert Liddell Lowe. *The New England Quarterly* (Brunswick, Maine), Vol. XXVII, pp. 257-261, June.

1955

EDWIN ARLINGTON ROBINSON AND ALANSON TUCKER SCHUMANN: A STUDY IN INFLUENCES, by Peter Dechert. *Dissertation Abstracts* (Ann Arbor, Michigan), Vol. XV, pp. 822-823.
EDWIN ARLINGTON ROBINSON, by Conrad Aiken. *The Times Literary Supplement* (London), October 14, p. 605.
EDWIN ARLINGTON ROBINSON'S PROPER NAMES, by William C. Childers. *Names: Journal of the American Name Society* (Berkeley, California), Vol. III, pp. 223-229, December.

1956

E. A. ROBINSON'S PRINCIPLES AND PRACTICE OF POETRY: THE EFFECTS OF HIS PRINCIPLES OF POETRY ON THE TECHNIQUE AND STRUCTURE OF THE POEMS, by Robert David Stevick. *Dissertation Abstracts* (Ann Arbor, Michigan), Vol. XVI, p. 2463.
WHAT'S IN A NAME? — OR IN A SIGNATURE? by Carl J. Weber. *MSS* (New York), Vol. VIII, pp. 185-188.

ON EDWIN ARLINGTON ROBINSON, by Conrad Aiken. *Colby Library Quarterly* (Waterville, Maine), Series IV, pp. 95-97, February.

ROBINSON'S "AMARYLLIS," by William C. Childers. *The Explicator* (Columbia, South Carolina), Vol. XIV, Item 34, February.

TO SEE ROBINSON, by Winfield Townley Scott. *The New Mexico Quarterly* (Albuquerque), Vol. XXVI, pp. 161-178, Summer.

WHAT IS A COLLECTOR'S ITEM: EMILY DICKINSON, E. A. ROBINSON, AND D. H. LAWRENCE? (AN ESSAY IN THE FORM OF A BIBLIOGRAPHY), by William White. *The American Book Collector* (Chicago), Vol. VI, pp. 6-8, Summer.

MORE LIGHT ON A SHADOWY FIGURE: A. H. LOUIS, THE ORIGINAL OF E. A. ROBINSON'S "CAPTAIN CRAIG," by Robert W. Hill. *Bulletin of the New York Public Library* (New York), Vol. LX, pp. 373-377, August.

1957

ORGANIC FORM IN THE SHORTER POEMS OF EDWIN ROBINSON ROBINSON, by Elmer Samuel Moon. *Dissertation Abstracts* (Ann Arbor, Michigan), Vol. XVII, p. 145.

PSYCHOLOGICAL ASPECTS OF THE POETRY OF EDWIN ARLINGTON ROBINSON, by Paul Hampton Morrill. *Dissertation Abstracts* (Ann Arbor, Michigan), Vol. XVII, pp. 363-364.

ROBINSON'S "EN PASSANT," by Bernice Slote. *The Explicator* (Columbia, South Carolina), Vol. XV, Item 27, February.

1958

ROBINSON'S "GAWAINE," by Jacob H. Adler. *English Studies* (Amsterdam), Vol. XXXIX, pp. 1-20, February.

POEMS PICKLED IN ANTHOLOGICAL BRINE, by Harry R. Garvin. *CEA Critic* (Saratoga Springs, New York), Vol. XX, pp. 1, 4 October. [On "Richard Cory."]

1959

ROBINSON AND WILLIAM JAMES, by Robert D. Stevick. *The University of Kansas City Review* (Kansas City, Missouri), Vol. XXV, pp. 293-301, June.

ROBINSON'S DARK-HILL-TO-CLIMB IMAGE, by Egbert S. Oliver. *Literary Criterion* (Mysore, India), Vol. III, pp. 36-52, Summer. [Reprinted in Mr. Oliver's *Studies in American Literature*, 1965.]

1960

EDWIN ARLINGTON ROBINSON AS DRAMATIST AND DRAMATIC POET, by Lucy Dickinson Fryxell. *Dissertation Abstracts* (Ann Arbor, Michigan), Vol. XX, pp. 4110-4111, April.

EDWIN ARLINGTON ROBINSON ON HIGHER EDUCATION, by Cecil D. Eby, Jr. *Colby Library Quarterly* (Waterville, Maine), Series V, pp. 163-164, September.

ROBINSON'S "RICHARD CORY," by Charles Burkhart. *The Explicator* (Columbia, South Carolina), Vol. XIX, Item 9, November.

IN MEMORIAM: EDWIN ARLINGTON ROBINSON [by Richard Cary.] *Colby Library Quarterly* (Waterville, Maine), Series V, p. 169, December. [See also, EDITOR'S EPILOGUE, p. 204.]

DOES IT MATTER HOW ANNANDALE WENT OUT? by David S. Nivison. *Colby Library Quarterly* (Waterville, Maine), Series V, pp. 170-185, December. [Reprinted in Richard Cary, *Appreciation* . . . See 1969, above.]

MOODY AND ROBINSON, by Maurice F. Brown. *Colby Library Quarterly* (Waterville, Maine), Series V, pp. 185-194, December.

ROBINSON'S NOTES TO HIS NIECES, by Richard Cary. *Colby Library Quarterly* (Waterville, Maine), Series V, pp. 195-202, December.

ROBINSON'S *TALIFER:* THE FIGURATIVE TEXTURE, by Richard Crowder. *Boston University Studies in English* (Boston), Vol. IV, pp. 241-247, Winter.

1961

EDWIN ARLINGTON ROBINSON, DISINHERITED PURITAN, by Lucy D. Sullivan. *The Gordon Review* (Wenham, Massachusetts), Vol. VI, No. 1, pp. 11-20, First issue, 1960-61.

THE FAILURE OF EDWIN ARLINGTON ROBINSON, by Richard P. Adams. *Tulane Studies in English* (New Orleans), Vol. XI, pp. 97-151.

IMAGE PATTERNS IN THE POETRY OF EDWIN ARLINGTON ROBINSON,
by Charles T. Davis. *College English* (Champaign, Illinois),
Vol. XXII, pp. 380-386, March. [Reprinted in Richard Cary,
Appreciation . . . See 1969, above.]

E. A. ROBINSON AND THE MEANING OF LIFE, by Richard Crowder.
The Chicago Review (Chicago), Vol. XV, pp. 5-17, Summer.

CHARACTER AND STRUCTURE IN EDWIN ARLINGTON ROBINSON'S
MAJOR NARRATIVES, by John Vail Foy. *Dissertation Abstracts*
(Ann Arbor, Michigan), Vol. XXII, p. 1996, December.

1962

THE ENGAGING MASK: ISOLATION IN THE EARLY POEMS OF EDWIN
ARLINGTON ROBINSON, by Joseph Fetler Malof. Doctoral
Dissertation, University of California at Los Angeles; see
Dissertation Abstracts (Ann Arbor, Michigan), Index 1961-1962,
Vol. XXII, p. 136.

REDEMPTION FOR THE MAN OF IRON, by Richard Crowder.
The Personalist (Los Angeles), Vol. XLIII, pp. 46-56, January.

ROBINSON'S "THE TREE IN PAMELA'S GARDEN," by Marvin Klotz.
The Explicator (Columbia, South Carolina), Vol. XX, Item 42,
January.

TWO VOICES OF THE AMERICAN VILLAGE: ROBINSON AND MASTERS,
by Robert N. Hertz. *Minnesota Review* (Minneapolis),
Vol. II, pp. 345-358, Spring.

COMPREHENSIVE CRITICISM: A HUMANISTIC DISCIPLINE, by Harry
R. Garvin. *Bucknell Review* (Lewisburg, Pennsylvania), Vol. X,
pp. 305-327, May. ["Richard Cory" is used as an example.]

A READING OF "MINIVER CHEEVY," by Laurence Perrine. *Colby
Library Quarterly* (Waterville, Maine), Series VI, pp. 65-74, June.

CONTEMPORARY REFERENCE TO ROBINSON'S ARTHURIAN POEMS,
by Laurence Perrine. *Twentieth Century Literature* (Denver), Vol.
VIII, pp. 74-82, July.

EDWIN ARLINGTON ROBINSON TO HARRIET MONROE: SOME
UNPUBLISHED LETTERS, by Robert Liddell Lowe. *Modern
Philology* (Chicago), Vol. LX, pp. 31-40, August.

UN GRAN PRECURSORE DI SPOON RIVER: EDWIN ARLINGTON ROBINSON
DOGANIERE DEL PESSIMISMO, by Paola Bompard. *La Fiera
Letteraria* (Rome, Italy), No. 36, p. 4, September 7.
SYMBOL AND THEME IN "MR. FLOOD'S PARTY," by James L. Allen,
Jr. *Mississippi Quarterly* (State College, Mississippi),
Vol. XV, pp. 139-143, Fall.
EDWIN ARLINGTON ROBINSON: A MUSICAL MEMOIR, by Mabel
Daniels. *Radcliffe Quarterly* (Cambridge, Massachusetts),
Vol. XLVI, pp. 5-11, November [Reprinted in *Colby Library
Quarterly* (Waterville, Maine), Series VI, pp. 219-233, June
1963.]
ROBINSON ON MOODY, by Richard Cary. *Colby Library Quarterly*
(Waterville, Maine), Series VI, pp. 176-183, December.

1963

ROBINSON'S "THE TREE IN PAMELA'S GARDEN," by Elizabeth Wright.
The Explicator (Columbia, South Carolina), Vol. XXI,
Item 47, February.
ROBINSON ON BROWNING, by Richard Cary. *Victorian Newsletter*
(New York), No. 23, pp. 19-21, Spring.
QUIET VOICES, UNQUIET TIMES, by Arthur M. Sampley. *Midwest
Quarterly* (Pittsburg, Kansas), Vol. III, pp. 247-256, Spring.
E. A. ROBINSON AS SOOTHSAYER, by Richard Cary. *Colby Library
Quarterly* (Waterville, Maine), Series VI, pp. 233-245, June.
[Reprinted in Richard Cary, *Appreciation* . . . See 1969, above.]
TOCQUEVILLE AS A SOURCE FOR ROBINSON'S "MAN AGAINST THE SKY,"
by Fred Somkin. *Colby Library Quarterly* (Waterville, Maine),
Series VI, pp. 245-247, June.
AVON'S HARVEST RE-EXAMINED, by Ronald Moran. *Colby Library
Quarterly* (Waterville, Maine), Series VI, pp. 247-254, June.
ROBINSON BONANZA [by Richard Cary]. *Colby Library Quarterly*
(Waterville, Maine), Series VI, p. 261, June. [About 54
Robinson letters to Arthur Davis Variell.]
EDWIN ARLINGTON ROBINSON: THE POETRY OF THE ACT, by
William Ronald Robinson. *Dissertation Abstracts* (Ann
Arbor, Michigan), Vol. XXIV, pp. 303-304, July.

78

ROBINSON'S "FIRELIGHT," by James D. Barry. *The Explicator* (Columbia, South Carolina), Vol. XXII, Item 21, November.

ROBINSON ON DICKENS, by Richard Cary. *American Notes & Queries* (New Haven, Connecticut), Vol. II, pp. 35-36, November.

THE APPEAL OF "RICHARD CORY," by David N. Rein. *CEA Critic* (Dallas, Texas), Vol. XXVI, p. 6, November.

A BRIEF DISCUSSION OF EDWIN ARLINGTON ROBINSON BASED ON HIS LIFE AND POETRY, by Wanne J. Joe. *The English Language and Literature* (English Literature Society of Korea, Seoul), No. 14, pp. 18-39.

1964

EDWIN ARLINGTON ROBINSON: POET OR VERSIFIER?, by James L. Allen, Jr. *English Record* (Binghamton, New York), Vol. XIV, pp. 9-15, February.

ROBINSON'S "DARK HILLS," by G. Thomas Tanselle. *CEA Critic* (Dallas, Texas), Vol. XXVI, pp. 8-10, February.

A LETTER OF EDWIN ARLINGTON ROBINSON TO JAMES BARSTOW, by Robert Liddell Lowe. *The New England Quarterly* (Brunswick, Maine), Vol. XXXVII, pp. 390-392, September.

LA POESIA DI EDWIN A. ROBINSON TRA OTTOCENTO E NOVECENTO, by Tommaso Pisanti. *Ausonia* (Siena, Italy), Vol. XIX, No. iv, pp. 32-35.

1965

A BIBLIOGRAPHY OF EDWIN ARLINGTON ROBINSON, 1941-1963, by William White. *Colby Library Quarterly* (Waterville, Maine), Series VII, pp. 1-26, March.

ROBINSON'S "RICHARD CORY," by Charles R. Morris. *The Explicator* (Columbia, South Carolina), Vol. XXIII, Item 52, March.

ROBINSON'S "LOST ANCHORS," by Ralph E. Jenkins. *The Explicator* (Columbia, South Carolina), Vol. XXIII, Item 64, April.

E. A. R.: A REMEMBRANCE, by Louis Untermeyer. *The Saturday Review* (New York), Vol. XLVIII, pp. 33-34, April 10.

E. A. ROBINSON'S SYSTEM OF OPPOSITES, by James G. Hepburn. *PMLA* (New York), Vol. LXXX, pp. 266-274, June. [Reprinted in Richard Cary, *Appreciation* . . . See 1969, above.]

E. A. ROBINSON'S POETICS, by Lewis E. Weeks, Jr. *Twentieth Century Literature* (Denver, Colorado), Vol. XI, pp. 131-145, October. [Reprinted in Richard Cary, *Appreciation* . . . See 1969, above.]

THE SHORTER POEMS OF THOMAS HARDY AND EDWIN ARLINGTON ROBINSON: A STUDY IN CONTRASTS, by Paul Nathan Zietlow. *Dissertation Abstracts* (Ann Arbor, Michigan), Vol. XXVI, p. 2765, November.

TILBURY TOWN (LETTURA DELLA POESIA DI EDWIN ARLINGTON ROBINSON), by Piero Mirizzi. *Annali della Facoltà di Lettere e Filosofia dell' Università di Bari* (Bari, Italy), Vol. X, pp. 217-279.

1966

E. A. ROBINSON E ROBERT FROST, by Claudio Gorlier. *Paragone* (Florence, Italy), N. S. Vol. XII, pp. 126-132, February.

E. A. ROBINSON'S USE OF EMERSON, by William J. Free. *American Literature* (Durham, North Carolina), Vol. XXXVIII, pp. 69-84, March.

WHERE IS E. A. ROBINSON?, by William White. *The American Book Collector* (Chicago), Vol. XVI, p. 7, March.

ROBINSON'S "LOST ANCHORS," by S. A. Cowan. *The Explicator* (Columbia, South Carolina), Vol. XXIV, Item 68, April.

THE HAPPY ENDING AS A CONTROLLING COMIC ELEMENT IN THE POETIC PHILOSOPHY OF EDWIN ARLINGTON ROBINSON, by Sara Louise Mott, *Dissertation Abstracts* (Ann Arbor, Michigan), Vol. XXVI, p. 6047, April.

THE ALIEN PITY: A STUDY OF CHARACTER IN E. A. ROBINSON'S POETRY, by Scott Donaldson. *American Literature* (Durham, North Carolina), Vol. XXXVIII, pp. 219-229. May.

E. A. R. IN INDIA, by William White. *The American Book Collector* (Chicago), Vol. XVI, p. 32, May.

STATEMENT AND POETRY, by Gerald E. Graff. *Southern Review* (Baton Rouge, Louisiana), N. S. Vol. II, pp. 499-515, Summer. [On Robinson's "Hillcrest."]

ROBINSON AND THE BIBLE, by Nicholas Ayo. *Dissertation Abstracts*
(Ann Arbor, Michigan), Vol. XXVII, pp. 469A-470A, August.
THE REHABILITATION OF EBEN FLOOD, by John E. Parish. *The English
Journal* (Champaign, Illinois), Vol. LV, pp. 696-699, September.
WITH FIRM ADDRESS: A CRITICAL STUDY OF 26 SHORTER POEMS OF
E. A. ROBINSON, by Ronald Wesson Moran, Jr. *Dissertation
Abstracts* (Ann Arbor, Michigan), Vol. XXVII, p. 1378A,
November.
ROBINSON'S "CAPTAIN CRAIG": A REINTERPRETATION, by Gertrude
M. White, *English Studies* (Amsterdam), Vol. XLVII,
pp. 432-439, December.

1967

E. A. ROBINSON'S "SCATTERED LIVES," by Wallace L. Anderson.
American Literature (Durham, North Carolina), Vol. XXXVIII,
pp. 498-507, January.
EDWIN ARLINGTON ROBINSON'S VIEW OF POETRY: A STUDY OF HIS
THEORY AND HIS TECHNIQUES IN THE LATE NARRATIVES,
by Nancy Carol Joyner. *Dissertation Abstracts* (Ann Arbor,
Michigan), Vol. XXVII, pp. 2531A-2532A, February.
THE LIBRARY OF EDWIN ARLINGTON ROBINSON: ADDENDA,
by Richard Cary. *Colby Library Quarterly* (Waterville, Maine),
Series VII, pp. 398-415, March.
E. A. ROBINSON'S "ANNANDALE" POEMS, by Charles Genthe. *Colby
Library Quarterly* (Waterville, Maine), Series VII,
pp. 392-398, March.
MEANING AND VALUE IN "LUKE HAVERGAL," by Ronald Moran.
Colby Library Quarterly (Waterville, Maine), Series VII,
pp. 385-391, March.
A NOTE ON ROBINSON'S "FORESTALLING," by J. S. Lewis. *American
Notes & Queries* (New Haven), Vol. V, p. 106, March.
THE MEANING OF TILBURY TOWN: ROBINSON AS A REGIONAL POET,
by Paul Zietlow. *The New England Quarterly* (Brunswick, Maine),
Vol. XL, pp. 188-211, June.

THE POWER OF SYMPATHY IN THE POETRY OF ROBINSON AND FROST:
THE "INSIDE" VS. THE "OUTSIDE" NARRATIVE, by Burton L. St.
Armand. *American Quarterly* (Philadelphia), Vol. XIX,
pp. 564-574, Fall.
THE SOURCES OF THE IMAGERY IN THE POETRY OF E. A. ROBINSON, by
Elise Dort Isley. *Dissertation Abstracts* (Ann Arbor, Michigan),
Vol. XXVIII, p. 1436A, October.
THE TORRENT AND THE NIGHT BEFORE [poem], by Carl W. Marr.
Colby Library Quarterly (Waterville, Maine), Series VII,
opp. p. 511, December.
"GO LITTLE BOOK": AN ODYSSEY OF ROBINSON'S *THE TORRENT
AND THE NIGHT BEFORE*, by Richard Cary. *Colby Library
Quarterly* (Waterville, Maine), Series VII, pp. 511-527, December.
TORRENTS COME IN DRIBLETS [by Richard Cary]. *Colby Library
Quarterly* (Waterville, Maine), Series VII, p. 548, December.
E. A. ROBINSON AND THE GARDEN OF EDEN, by Richard Crowder.
Colby Library Quarterly (Waterville, Maine), Series VII,
pp. 527-535, December.
ROBINSON'S "FOR A DEAD LADY": AN EXERCISE IN EVALUATION,
by Clyde L. Grimm. *Colby Library Quarterly* (Waterville, Maine),
Series VII, pp. 535-547, December. [Reprinted in Richard Cary,
Appreciation . . . See 1969, above.]
ROBINSON ON VERLAINE, by C. Subbian. *American Studies Research
Centre Newsletter* (Hyderabad, India), No. 11, pp. 52-54,
December.

1968

NARRATIVE FORM IN THE LONG POEMS OF EDWIN ARLINGTON
ROBINSON, by Richard Samuel Moseley, III. *Dissertation Abstracts*
(Ann Arbor, Michigan), Vol XXVIII, p. 3193A, February.
ROBINSON'S "THE MAN AGAINST THE SKY," by Arthur M. Read, II.
The Explicator (Richmond, Virginia), Vol. XXVI, Item 49,
February.
METAPHOR AND IMAGERY IN E. A. ROBINSON'S "CREDO," by Richard
G. Landini. *Colby Library Quarterly* (Waterville, Maine),
Series VIII, pp. 20-22, March.

EDWIN ARLINGTON ROBINSON: A BRIEF BIOGRAPHY, by J. V.
Cunningham, *Denver Quarterly* (Denver, Colorado), Vol. III,
pp. 28-31, Spring.

EDWIN ARLINGTON ROBINSON'S "AMARANTH": A JOURNEY TO "THE
WRONG WORLD," by Dolores E. Brien. *Research Studies of
Washington State University* (Pullman, Washington),
Vol. XXXVI, pp. 143-150, June.

THEODORE ROOSEVELT AND EDWIN ARLINGTON ROBINSON:
A COMMON VISION, by David H. Burton. *The Personalist* (Los
Angeles), Vol. XLIX, pp. 331-350, Summer.

ROBINSON'S MODERNITY, by J. C. Levenson. *Virginia Quarterly
Review* (Charlottesville, Virginia), Vol. XLIV, pp. 590-610,
Autumn. [Reprinted in Ellsworth Barnard, *Centenary* . . . See 1969,
above; and in Francis Murphy, *A Collection* . . . See 1969, above.]

EDWIN ARLINGTON ROBINSON'S "THE SHEAVES," by Mary S. Mattfield.
CEA Critic (Saratoga Springs, New York). Vol. XXXI, p. 10,
November.

SOME PURITAN CHARACTERISTICS OF THE POETRY OF EDWIN
ARLINGTON ROBINSON, by James Anthony Gowen. *Dissertation
Abstracts* (Ann Arbor, Michigan), Vol. XXIX, pp. 1538A-1539A,
November.

THE *MAKARIS* OF CAMELOT, by Celia B. Morris. *Dissertation
Abstracts* (Ann Arbor, Michigan), Vol. XXIX, pp. 1516A-1517A,
November.

1969

ROBINSON'S "FLAMMONDE," by Hilton Anderson. *Southern Review*
(Baton Rouge, Louisiana), Vol. VII, pp. 179-183, January.

ROBINSON'S PAMELA AND SANDBURG'S AGATHA, by Nancy Joyner.
American Literature (Durham, North Carolina), Vol. XL, pp.
548-549, January.

ROBINSON'S USE OF THE BIBLE, by Nicholas Ayo. *Colby Library
Quarterly* (Waterville, Maine), Series VIII, pp. 250-265, March.
[Reprinted in Richard Cary, *Appreciation* . . . See 1969, above.]

ROBINSON, ROOSEVELT, AND ROMANISM: AN HISTORICAL REFLECTION OF THE CATHOLIC CHURCH AND THE AMERICAN IDEAL, by David H. Burton. *Records of the American Catholic Historical Society of Philadelphia* (Philadelphia), Vol. LXXX, pp. 3-16, March.

ROBINSON BOOKS AND PERIODICALS: I, by Richard Cary. *Colby Library Quarterly* (Waterville, Maine), Series VIII, pp. 266-277, March.

TWO CORYS: A SAMPLE OF INDUCTIVE TEACHING, by Linda J. Clifton. *English Journal* (Champaign, Illinois), Vol. LVIII, pp. 414-415, March.

ROBINSON'S REPUTATION: SIX OBSERVATIONS, by Richard Crowder. *Colby Library Quarterly* (Waterville, Maine), Series VIII, pp. 220-238, March.

ROBINSON'S IMPULSE FOR NARRATIVE, by J. Vail Foy. *Colby Library Quarterly* (Waterville, Maine), Series VIII, pp. 238-249, March. [Reprinted in Richard Cary, *Appreciation* . . . See 1969, above.]

ON REREADING ROBINSON, by Archibald MacLeish, *Colby Library Quarterly* (Waterville, Maine), Series VIII, pp. 217-219, March. [Reprinted in Richard Cary, *Appreciation* . . . See 1969, above.]

ROBINSON'S "BATTLE AFTER WAR," by Dean Sherman. *The Explicator* (Richmond, Virginia), Vol. XXVIII, Item 64, April.

UN DESTIN BIZAR: EDWIN ARLINGTON ROBINSON, by Petre Solomon. *România Literara* (Bucharest, Romania), June 19, p. 23.

E. A. ROBINSON'S IDEA OF GOD, by David H. Burton. *Colby Library Quarterly* (Waterville, Maine), Series VIII, pp. 280-294, June. [Reprinted in Richard Cary, *Appreciation* . . . See 1969, above.]

ROBINSON BOOKS AND PERIODICALS: II, by Richard Cary. *Colby Library Quarterly* (Waterville, Maine), Series VIII, pp. 334-343, June.

TWO ROBINSON REVISIONS: "MR. FLOOD'S PARTY" AND "THE DARK HILLS," by Louise Dauner. *Colby Library Quarterly* (Waterville, Maine), Series VIII, pp. 309-310, June.

FORMULATION OF E. A. ROBINSON'S PRINCIPLES OF POETRY, by Robert D. Stevick. *Colby Library Quarterly* (Waterville, Maine), Series VIII, pp. 295-308, June. [Reprinted in Richard Cary, *Appreciation* . . . See 1969, above.]

EDWIN ARLINGTON ROBINSON, by Mark Van Doren. *Colby Library Quarterly* (Waterville, Maine), Series VIII, p. 279, June.

MAINE IN THE POETRY OF EDWIN ARLINGTON ROBINSON, by Lewis E. Weeks, Jr. *Colby Library Quarterly* (Waterville, Maine) Series VIII, pp. 317-334, June.

THREE MEETINGS WITH ROBINSON, by Conrad Aiken. *Colby Library Quarterly* (Waterville, Maine), Series VIII, pp. 345-346, September.

ROBINSON BOOKS AND PERIODICALS: III, by Richard Cary. *Colby Library Quarterly* (Waterville, Maine), Series VIII, pp. 399-413, September.

HE SHOUTS TO SEE THEM SCAMPER SO: E. A. ROBINSON AND THE FRENCH FORMS, by Peter Dechert. *Colby Library Quarterly* (Waterville, Maine), Series VIII, pp. 386-398, September. [Reprinted in Richard Cary, *Appreciation* . . . See 1969, above.]

AN UNPUBLISHED VERSION OF "MR. FLOOD'S PARTY," by Nancy Joyner. *English Language Notes* (Boulder, Colorado, Vol. VII, pp. 55-57, September.

THE OCTAVES OF E. A. ROBINSON, by Ronald Moran. *Colby Library Quarterly* (Waterville, Maine), Series VIII, pp. 363-370, September. [Reprinted in Richard Cary, *Appreciation* . . . See 1969, above.]

E. A. ROBINSON'S YANKEE CONSCIENCE, by W. R. Robinson. *Colby Library Quarterly* (Waterville, Maine), Series VIII, pp. 371-385, September. [Reprinted in Richard Cary, *Appreciation* . . . See 1969, above.]

THE PLAYS OF EDWIN ARLINGTON ROBINSON, by Irving D. Suss. *Colby Library Quarterly* (Waterville, Maine), Series VIII, pp. 347-363, September. [Reprinted in Richard Cary, *Appreciation* . . . See 1969, above.]

ROBINSON'S "VETERAN SIRENS," by Brian M. Barbour. *The Explicator* (Richmond, Virginia), Vol. XXVIII, Item 20, November.

ROBINSON MANUSCRIPTS AND LETTERS, by Richard Cary. *Colby Library Quarterly* (Waterville, Maine), Series VIII, pp. 479-487, December.

FATE, TRAGEDY AND PESSIMISM IN ROBINSON'S "MERLIN," by Lyle Domina. *Colby Library Quarterly* (Waterville, Maine), Series VIII, pp. 471-478, December.

Edwin Arlington Robinson and the Theatre of Destiny, by
Michael C. Hinden. *Colby Library Quarterly* (Waterville,
Maine), Series VIII, pp. 463-471, December.

"The World Is . . . A Kind of Spiritual Kindergarten," by Paul
H. Morrill. *Colby Library Quarterly* (Waterville, Maine), Series
VIII, pp. 435-448, December. [Reprinted in Richard Cary,
Appreciation . . . See 1969, above.]

Tennyson and Robinson: Legalistic Moralism vs. Situation
Ethics, by Laurence Perrine. *Colby Library Quarterly* (Waterville,
Maine), Series VIII, pp. 416-433, December.

Simon Simple, by Louis Untermeyer. *Colby Library Quarterly*
(Waterville, Maine), Series VIII, p. 415, December.

A Bibliography of Edwin Arlington Robinson, 1964-1969, by
William White. *Colby Library Quarterly* (Waterville, Maine),
Series VIII, pp. 448-462, December.

The Intellectualism of Edwin Arlington Robinson, by David
H. Burton. *Thought* (Bronx, New York), Vol. XLIV, pp.
565-580, Winter.

1970

Edwin Arlington Robinson as Social Critic and Moral Guide,
by John Cashion Bierk. *Dissertation Abstracts International* (Ann
Arbor, Michigan), Vol. XXX, pp. 2997A-2998A, January.

Major Categories of Irony in the Poetry of Edwin Arlington
Robinson, by Leon James Satterfield. *Dissertation Abstracts
International* (Ann Arbor, Michigan), Vol. XXX, p. 3022A
January.

E. A. Robinson and Henry Cabot Lodge, by John W. Crowley.
The New England Quarterly (Brunswick, Maine), Vol. XLIII,
pp. 115-124, March.

Robinson's "Richard Cory," by Steven Turner. *The Explicator*
(Richmond, Virginia), Vol. XXVIII, Item 73, May.

Broceliande: E. A. Robinson's Palace of Art, by W. R. Thompson.
The New England Quarterly (Brunswick, Maine), Vol. LXIII,
pp. 231-249, June.

TRIBUTE TO AN AMERICAN POET, by Irving Howe. *Harper's Magazine* (New York), Vol. CCXL, pp. 103-108, June. [See article below.]

BOOKS: AMPLIFICATION, by Scott Donaldson. *Harper's Magazine* (New York), Vol. CCXLI, p. 9, September. [Corrects Irving Howe, above.]

REMEMBER E. A. ROBINSON, by William White. *Literary Sketches* (Williamsburg, Virginia), Vol. X, pp. 8-9, September.

C. Reviews of Individual Books

The Torrent and the Night Before

[THE TORRENT AND THE NIGHT BEFORE]. *Time and the Hour*
(Boston), Vol. IV, pp. 10-11, December 26, 1896.

The Children of the Night (1897)

EDWARD [*sic.*] ARLINGTON ROBINSON, by Edith Brower. *Wilkes-Barre*
Times (Wilkes-Barre, Pennsylvania), December 20, 1897, p. 15.
[Reprinted in *Letters to Edith Brower*, 1968, pp. 216-224.]

GOOD VERSE. *The Hartford Post* (Hartford, Connecticut),
January 6, 1898, p. 8.

Captain Craig (1902)

In article entitled WHAT BOOK FOLK OF BOSTON AND NEW YORK
ARE TALKING ABOUT, by J[ohn] A[lbert] Macy. *The Chicago*
Evening Post (Chicago), October 25, 1902, p. 9.

In article entitled MOST RECENT VERSE BY AMERICAN SINGERS.
The Chicago Evening Post (Chicago), December 6, 1902, p. 16.

The Children of the Night (1905)

THE CHILDREN OF THE NIGHT. *The Dial* (Chicago), Vol. XXXIX,
p. 314, November 16, 1905.

ROBINSON: THE CHILDREN OF THE NIGHT. *The Critic* (New York),
Vol. XLVII, p. 584, December 1905.

In article entitled VOLUMES OF POEMS AND BOOKS ON POETRY.
The American Monthly Review of Reviews (New York),
Vol. XXXIII, p. 122, January 1906.

The Town Down the River

In article entitled RECENT VERSE. *The Nation* (New York), Vol. XCII,
    p. 11, January 5, 1911.
THE TOWN DOWN THE RIVER. *The Independent* (New York),
    Vol. LXX, p. 470, March 2, 1911.

Captain Craig (1915)

CAPT. CRAIG. *The Evening Sun*, New York, April 17, 1915, p. 7.
In article entitled TWO POETS OF THE DAY. *The American Review
    of Reviews* (New York), Vol. LI, p. 632, May 1915.

Van Zorn

A DIFFERENCE OF OPINION. *The Independent* (New York),
    Vol. LXXX, p. 141, October 26, 1914.
EDWIN ARLINGTON ROBINSON, by W[illiam] S[tanley] B[raithwaite].
    The Cornhill Booklet (Boston), Vol. IV, pp. 90-91,
    December 1914.
VAN ZORN, by Homer E. Woodbridge. *The Dial* (Chicago),
    Vol. LVIII, p. 48, January 16, 1915.
VAN ZORN. *The Nation* (New York), Vol. C, p. 205, February 18,
    1915.

The Porcupine

THE PORCUPINE: A DRAMA IN THREE ACTS. *Cleveland Open Shelf*
    (Cleveland, Ohio), October 1915, p. 93.
THE BRISTLING WIFE. *The Evening Sun* (New York), November 13,
    1915, p. 9.

The Man Against the Sky

"— AND OTHER POEMS," by Louis Untermeyer. *The Chicago Evening
    Post* (Chicago), March 10, 1916, p. 11.
In article entitled CURRENT POETRY, *The Literary Digest* (New York),
    Vol. LII, p. 738, March 18, 1916.
In article entitled SOME NEW POETRY. *The American Review of
    Reviews* (New York), Vol. LIII, p. 632, May 1916.

THE MAN AGAINST THE SKY, by Raymond M. Alden. *The Dial*
(Chicago), Vol. LXI, pp. 62-63, July 15, 1916.

Merlin

In article entitled RECENT POETRY: POETS WHO ADHERE TO RHYME.
The American Review of Reviews (New York), Vol. LV,
p. 660, June 1917.

Lancelot

ROBINSON'S "LANCELOT," by Herbert S[herman] Gorman. *The
Evening Post Book Review* (New York), April 17, 1920, p. 5.

ROBINSON'S "LANCELOT," by Clement Wood. *The Call Magazine—
Supplement to the New York Call* (New York), May 16,
1920, p. 11.

E. A. ROBINSON'S FINE "LANCELOT," by Llewellyn Jones. *The Chicago
Evening Post* (Chicago), May 21, 1920, p. 9.

LANCELOT. *The Dial* (Chicago), Vol. LXIX, p. 103, July 1920.

LANCELOT, A POEM. *Cleveland Open Shelf* (Cleveland, Ohio),
October 1920, p. 86.

In article entitled ANTHOLOGISTS AND POETS, by Edward Bliss Reed.
The Yale Review (New Haven), Vol. VI, pp. 205-206,
October 1920.

The Three Taverns

EDWIN ARLINGTON ROBINSON DEFINES AND ILLUSTRATES POETRY,
by Edwin Carty Ranck. *The New York Herald Magazine and
Books* (New York), January 2, 1921, p. 10.

SOBER AS THE TIME, by C.F.G. *The Grinnell Review* (Grinnell, Iowa),
Vol. XVI, p. 332, January 1921.

Avon's Harvest

AVON'S HARVEST. *Grinnell Review* (Grinnell, Iowa), Vol. XVI,
p. 455, June 1921.

BLANK VERSE TALE OF HATE AND FEAR, by Edwin Carty Ranck.
   The New York Herald Magazine and Books (New York),
   June 5, 1921, p. 12.
AVON'S HARVEST. *The Dial* (New York), Vol. LXXI, p. 243,
   August 1921.

Collected Poems (1921)

COLLECTED POEMS. *The Literary Digest* (New York), Vol. LXXI,
   p. 38, December 24, 1921.
AN AMERICAN POET. *The Outlook* (London), Vol. L, pp. 175-176,
   August 26, 1922.
AN AMERICAN MASTER-POET, by E[dward] B[olland] Osborn.
   The Morning Post (London), November 3, 1922, p. 6.
AMERICAN POET'S VERSE MOST ENDURING IN ENGLISH LITERATURE
   THE PAST YEAR. *National Magazine* (Boston). Vol. LI, p. 285,
   November 1922.

Roman Bartholow

TRAGEDY. *The New York Herald Books* (New York), April 8,
   1923, p. 14.
In article entitled NEW BOOKS AND OLD, by M.L.F. *The Independent*
   (New York), Vol. CX, p. 319, May 12, 1923.

The Man Who Died Twice

In article entitled THE BLOOMIN' LYRE, by Arthur Guiterman.
   The Outlook (New York), Vol. CXXVI, p. 649, April 16, 1924.
In article entitled RECENT VERSE, by E[mily] B[eatrix] C[oursolles]
   Jones. *The Nation and the Athenaeum* (London), Vol. XXXV,
   pp. 248, 250, May 24, 1924.
LOST: A WIFE AND A GENIUS, by E[dward] A. Weeks. *The
   Independent* (Boston), Vol. CXIII, p. 20, July 5, 1924.
POETRY: THE MAN WHO DIED TWICE. *The Times Literary Supplement*
   (London), No. 1183, September 18, 1924, p. 582.
A NOVELIST AND A POET VISIT SPOON RIVER, by May Sinclair and
   Robert Nichols. [*The Literary Digest*] *International Book Review*
   (New York), Vol. III, pp. 32-33, 66-67, December 1924.

Dionysus in Doubt

POET'S OFFERINGS: ROBINSON INDIGNANT, SADDENED, by Joseph
Auslander. *The World* (New York), April 26, 1925, p. 7m.
In article entitled NEW BOOKS IN BRIEF REVIEW. *The Independent*
(Boston), Vol. CXIV, p. 563, May 16, 1925.
In article entitled PARNASUS AND THEREABOUT, by Arthur Guiterman.
The Outlook (New York), Vol. CXL, p. 112, May 20, 1925.
DIONYSUS IN DOUBT, by Grace Hazard Conkling. *The North American
Review* (New York), Vol. CCXXII, pp. 159-160, September-
October-December 1925.
In article entitled A NOTE ON RECENT AMERICAN VERSE, by
Edward Bliss Reed. *The Yale Review* (New Haven), Vol. XV,
pp. 811-812, July 1926.
THIS "UNRANSOMED JUVENILE MISCALLED DEMOCRACY," by Percy A.
Hutchinson. *Current Reviews*, edited by Lewis Worthington
Smith. New York: Henry Holt & Company, 1926, pp. 308-314.
Reprinted from *The New York Times Book Review* (New York),
March 29, 1925, p. 5.

Tristram

In article entitled NEW BOOKS IN BRIEF REVIEW. *The Independent*
(Boston), Vol. CXVII, p. 448, April 23, 1927.
In article entitled THE MUSES OUT OF WORK, by Edmund Wilson.
The New Republic (New York), Vol. L, p. 319, May 11, 1927.
In article entitled SCRIPTS FOR SUMMER SOLSTICE, by Leon Whipple.
The Survey (New York), Vol. LVIII, p. 390, July 1, 1927.
TRISTRAM. *The Dial* (New York), Vol. LXXXIII, p. 174, August 1927.
FOR THOSE WHO LOVE POETRY, by Emily Blair Newell. *Good
Housekeeping* (New York), Vol. LXXXV, pp. 208-209,
December 1927.

Collected Poems (1927)

In article entitled BOOKS IN BRIEF. *The Nation* (New York),
Vol. CXXVI, p. 169, February 8, 1928.

Sonnets 1889-1927

In article entitled POETRY FROM FOUR MEN, by George O'Neill.
The Outlook and Independent (New York), Vol. CLI, p. 111,
January 16, 1929.
EDWIN ARLINGTON ROBINSON: SONNETS, by C[harles] Cestre.
Revue Anglo-Américaine (Paris), Vol. VI, pp. 377-378,
April 1929.
SONNETS. *Poetry* (Chicago), Vol. XXXIV, pp. 114-115, May 1929.

Cavender's House

CAVENDER'S HOUSE, by W.E.G. *The Christian Century* (Chicago),
Vol. XLV, p. 618, May 8, 1929.
In article entitled BOOKS IN BRIEF. *The Nation* (New York),
Vol. CXXVIII, p. 567, May 8, 1929.
CAVENDER'S HOUSE, by T[heodore] H[oward] Banks, Jr. *The Cardinal*
(Wesleyan University, Middletown, Connecticut), Vol. IV,
pp. 29-31, June 1929.
MAN, WOMAN, AND POETRY: CAVENDER'S HOUSE, by Oakley Johnson.
The Book League Monthly (New York), Vol. II, pp. 183-184,
July 1929.
In article entitled SOME RECENT BOOKS OF POETRY, by Newton Arvin.
The Atlantic Monthly (Boston), Vol. CXLIV, The Atlantic
Bookshelf, p. 20, July 1929.

The Glory of the Nightingales

"TO UNDERSTAND IS TO FORGIVE" [by Howard Edward Balme
Speight]. *The Christian Leader* (Boston), N.S. Vol. XXXIII,
pp. 1412-1413, November 8, 1930.
THE GLORY OF THE NIGHTINGALES. *Pittsburgh Monthly Bulletin*
(Pittsburgh), Vol. XXXV, p. 82, November 1930.
GLORY OF THE NIGHTINGALES, by Frank B[rown] Stover. *The
Wesleyan Cardinal* (Middletown, Connecticut), Vol. VI,
pp. 28-30, November 1930.
A POETIC MELODRAMA, by Raymond Kresensky. *The Christian Century*
(Chicago), Vol. XLVII, p. 1595, December 24, 1930.

Matthias at the Door

OLD MASTER, *Time* (New York), Vol. XVIII, p. 71, October 12, 1931.
MATTHIAS AT THE DOOR. *Pittsburgh Monthly Bulletin* (Pittsburgh),
Vol. XXXVI, p. 86, December 1931.
AN INTERREGNUM OF GENIUS, by Joseph Lewis French. *The
Commonweal* (New York), Vol. XV, p. 412, February 10, 1932.
In article entitled THREE VOLUMES WORTH READING, by George St.
Clair. *The New Mexico Quarterly* (Albuquerque), Vol. II,
pp. 92-93, February 1932.

Nicodemus

ROBINSON ITEM. *Time* (New York), Vol. XX, p. 44, October 10, 1932.
NICODEMUS, by Johnston Beech. *The Churchman* (New York), Vol.
CXLVI, p. 5, October 15, 1932.
E. A. ROBINSON PRESENTS NEW BOOK OF POEMS, by Fanny Butcher.
Chicago Tribune (Chicago), Section I, p. 10, October 22, 1932.
In article entitled SHORTER NOTICES. *The Nation* (New York),
Vol. CXXXV, p. 407, October 26, 1932.
I'D RATHER READ POETRY, by Henry Davis Nadig. *New Canaan
Advertiser* (New Canaan, Connecticut), October 27, 1932, p. 9.
POETRY THAT IS NOT SONG. *The Christian Century* (Chicago),
Vol. XLIX, pp. 1347-1348, November 2, 1932.
In article entitled ROUND ABOUT PARNASUS: TWO VETERANS,
by William Rose Benét. *The Saturday Review of Literature*
(New York), Vol. IX, p. 224, November 5, 1932.
NICODEMUS. *The Times Literary Supplement* (London), No. 1611,
December 15, 1932, p. 966.
NICODEMUS, *Pittsburgh Monthly Bulletin* (Pittsburgh), Vol. XXXVII,
p. 78, December 1932.
In article entitled POETRY IN A TIME OF DOUBT, by Odell Shepard.
The Yale Review (New Haven), Vol. XXII, p. 593, March 1933.

Talifer

TALIFER, by Virginia Barney. *The North American Review* (New
York), Vol. CCXXII, p. iv, January 1934.

TALIFER, by M.L.W. *The English Journal* (Chicago), Vol. XXIII, p. 677, October 1934.

Amaranth

ROBINSONIAN AVERNUS, by Isabel Foster. *The Christian Science Monitor* (Boston), September 26, 1934, p. 14.

POEMS: ROBINSON PRESENTS HIS TWENTY-THIRD BOOK OF VERSE. *News-Week* (Dayton, Ohio), Vol. IV, p. 39, September 29, 1934.

In article entitled POETS OLD & NEW. *Time* (New York), Vol. XXIV, pp. 62-63, October 1, 1934.

A PAGE ABOUT POETS: AMARANTH, by Ruth Lechlitner. *The New Republic* (New York), Vol. LXXX, p. 282, October 17, 1934.

THE LATEST ROBINSON, by John Haynes Holmes. *Unity* (Chicago), Vol. CXIV, pp. 95-96, October 29, 1934.

LEVITATION BY BOOTSTRAP, by Llewellyn Jones. *The Midwest* (Chicago), Vol. I, pp. 1, 7, November 1934.

"MISHANDLED HERITAGE," by Rabbi Victor E[manuel] Reichert. *The American Israelite* (Cincinnati), Vol. LXXXI, p. 4, December 27, 1934.

AMARANTH, by Raymond Larsson. *The Commonweal* (New York), Vol. XXI, p. 349, January 18, 1935.

AMARANTH. *The English Journal* (Chicago), Vol. XXIV, p. 173, February 1935.

King Jasper

POET'S CORNER: E. A. ROBINSON. *News-Week* (Dayton, Ohio), Vol. VI, p. 47, November 16, 1935.

PRINCE OF HEARTACHERS. *The Times Literary Supplement* (London), No. 1774, February 1, 1936, p. 91.

In article entitled SOCIETY AND SOLITUDE IN POETRY, by F[rancis] O. Matthiessen, *The Yale Review* (New Haven), Vol. XXV, pp. 603-604, March 1936.

KING JASPER: A POEM, by Mildred Boie. *The New England Quarterly*, (Norwood, Massachusetts), Vol. IX, pp. 154-156, March 1936.

KING JASPER: A POSTHUMOUS POEM, by Joseph Auslander. *The North American Review* (New York), Vol. CCXLI, pp. 375-376, June 1936.

KING JASPER, by Lascelles Abercrombie. *Modern Language Notes* (Baltimore), Vol. LII, pp. 218-220, March 1937.

Collected Poems (1937)

THE FIRST CITIZEN OF TILBURY TOWN, by Alexander M. Buchan. *St. Louis Post-Dispatch* (St. Louis), April 25, 1937, Section H, p. 4.

E. A. ROBINSON, by Russell Smith. *The Washington Post* (Washington, D. C.), May 2, 1937, Part III, p. 7.

A WORLD HIS OWN, by John Kenneth Merton. *The Commonweal* (New York), Vol. XXVI, pp. 79-80, May 14, 1937.

ROBINSON, POET OF AMERICA, by I[sabel] F[oster]. *The Christian Science Monitor Weekly Magazine Section* (Boston), May 26, 1937, p. 10.

THE COMPLETE ROBINSON, by Percy H[olmes] Boynton. *The New Republic* (New York), Vol. XCI, pp. 314-315, July 21, 1937.

ROBINSON: THE IRONIC DISCIPLINE, by Morton Dauwen Zabel. *The Nation* (New York), Vol. CXLV, pp. 222-223, August 28, 1937.

In article entitled POETRY IN 1937, by Horace Gregory. *New Masses Literary Supplement* (New York), Vol. XXV, p. 12, December 7, 1937.

Selected Letters

ROBINSON'S LETTERS TO HIS FRIENDS, by J[ohn] D[ynes] W[eaver]. *The Kansas City Star* (Kansas City, Missouri), February 24, 1940, p. 14.

A POET'S LETTERS, by Edward N[athaniel] Jenckes. *The Springfield Daily Republican* (Springfield, Massachusetts), February 24, 1940, p. 6.

COOL INTELLIGENT ASTRINGENCE, by Arthur Davison Ficke. *New York Herald Tribune Books* (New York), February 25, 1940, p. 6.

Edwin Arlington Robinson as Seen in His Letters, by Percy
Hutchison. *The New York Times Book Review* (New York),
February 25, 1940, p. 5.

Robinson, by W[infield] T[ownley] S[cott]. *The Providence Sunday
Journal*, (Providence, Rhode Island), February 25, 1940,
Part VI, p. 6.

Fitful Glimpses, by Louis Untermeyer. *The Saturday Review of
Literature* (New York), Vol. XXI, p. 7, March 2, 1940.

E. A. Robinson, by Anne Buckalew. *Daily Times Herald* (Dallas,
Texas), March 3, 1940, Part III, p. 16.

Foiled Circuitous Wanderer, by E[dward] Merrill Root. *The
Christian Century* (Chicago), Vol. LVII, p. 316, March 6, 1940.

A Poet to His Friends, by Harold D[avid] Carew. *Pasadena Star-
News* (Pasadena, California), March 16, 1940, Part II, p. 24.

Books and Book Folks, by Harold T[rowbridge] Pulsifer. *Portland
Press-Herald* (Portland, Maine), March 23, 1940, p. 5.

Edwin Arlington Robinson, by Mowry Saben. *The Argonaut*
(San Francisco), Vol. CXIX, pp. 21-22, March 29, 1940.

'Dear Friends, Reproach Me Not . . . ,' by John Ritchey. *The
Christian Science Monitor Weekly Magazine Section* (Boston),
March 30, 1940, p. 11.

The "Long Animal," by F[rederick] W[ilcox] Dupee. *The Nation*
(New York), Vol. CL, pp. 427-428, March 30, 1940.

Moon's Other Side, by Isobel Griscom. *The Chattanooga Daily Times
Magazine Section* (Chattanooga, Tennessee), April 7, 1940,
p. 5.

Selected Letters, by T[heodore] M[aynard]. *The Catholic World*
(New York), Vol. CLI, pp. 248-249, May 1940.

In article entitled New Light on Some Literary Lives, by Archibald
A[nderson] Hill. *The Virginia Quarterly Review* (Charlottesville,
Virginia), Vol. XVI, pp. 454-455, Summer 1940.

Faith of E. A. Robinson. *The Times Literary Supplement* (London),
No. 2012, p. 412, August 24, 1940.

Selected Letters of Edwin Arlington Robinson, by John Finch.
The New England Quarterly (Orono, Maine), Vol. XIII,
pp. 733-735, December 1940.

SELECTED LETTERS OF EDWIN ARLINGTON ROBINSON, by James
   Southall Wilson. *American Literature* (Durham, North Carolina),
   Vol. XII, pp. 512-514, January 1941.
FAITH IN THE PIECES, by Frances Wentworth Knickerbocker.
   The Sewanee Review (Sewanee, Tennessee), Vol. XLIX,
   pp. 125-126, January-March 1941.

Edwin Arlington Robinson: A Biography,
   by Hermann Hagedorn

DEMANDS OF POETRY RULED LIFE OF EDWIN ARLINGTON ROBINSON,
   by J[ohn] D[ynes] W[eaver]. *The Kansas City Star* (Kansas
   City, Missouri), October 4, 1938, p. 28.
BOOKS OF THE TIMES, by Ralph Thompson. *The New York Times*
   (New York), October 4, 1938, p. 19.
BOOKS AND THINGS, by Lewis Gannett, *New York Herald Tribune*
   (New York), October 5, 1938, p. 15.
ROBINSON REVEALED BY THE INTANGIBLES OF A TROUBLED SOUL,
   by Howard Mumford Jones. *Boston Evening Transcript* (Boston),
   October 8, 1938, Section 3, p. 1.
HAGEDORN'S BIOGRAPHY OF POET ROBINSON IS READY, by Alice
   Frost Lord. *Lewiston Journal Illustrated Magazine Section*
   (Lewiston, Maine), October 8, 1938, p. 9.
UNFINISHED PORTRAIT, by Louis Untermeyer. *The Saturday Review of
   Literature* (New York), Vol. XVIII, p. 34, October 15, 1938.
A REVEALING BIOGRAPHY OF E. A. ROBINSON, by Percy Hutchison.
   The New York Times Book Review (New York),
   October 16, 1938, p. 5.
TO BE POET IS MORE THAN TO WRITE VERSE, by Richard Bradley
   Koster. *The Christian Register* (Boston), Vol. CXVII, p. 606,
   October 20, 1938.
BIOGRAPHY OF ROBINSON RECALLS TOUR OF PUBS, by John Cournos.
   New Haven Sunday Register (New Haven), October 23, 1938,
   Part IV, p. 5.
A POET'S LIFE, by Eda Lou Walton. *The Nation* (New York),
   Vol. CXLVII, p. 460, October 29, 1938.

A POET WHO NEVER BELIEVED IN SUCCESS, by Horace Gregory.
  New York Herald Tribune Books (New York), October 30,
  1938, p. 7.
A FRIEND TELLS THE STORY OF A MAN BORN TO BE A POET,
  by Madeline Mason. *The Sun* (New York), October 31, 1938,
  p. 26.
PRINCE OF CASTAWAYS, by E[dward] Merrill Root. *The Christian
  Century* (Chicago), Vol. LV, p. 1337, November 2, 1938.
THE CASTLE OF DOUBT, by Robert Morss Lovett. *The New Republic*
  (New York), Vol. XCVII, pp. 107-108, November 30, 1938.
EDWIN ARLINGTON ROBINSON, A BIOGRAPHY, by Odell Shepard.
  The Key Reporter (New York), Vol. IV, p. 7, Winter 1939.
DEVIL'S ADVOCATE, by William Norman Guthrie. *The Churchman*
  (New York), Vol. CLIII, p. 5, May 15, 1939.
ROBINSON TO ROBINSON, by Winfield Townley Scott. *Poetry* (Chicago)
  Vol. LIV, pp. 92-100, May 1939.
EDWIN ARLINGTON ROBINSON, A BIOGRAPHY, by Mildred Boie.
  The New England Quarterly (Orono, Maine), Vol. XII,
  pp. 390-393, June 1939.
A POET WHO WAS LESS THAN HIS POEMS, by Robert P. Tristram
  Coffin. *Yankee* (Dublin, New Hampshire), Vol. V, pp. 4-5,
  June 1939.
EDWIN ARLINGTON ROBINSON, by C[harles] Cestre. *Études Anglaises*
  (Paris), Vol. III, pp. 304-305, July-September 1939.
EDWIN ARLINGTON ROBINSON: A BIOGRAPHY, by F. O. Matthiessen.
  American Literature (Durham, North Carolina), Vol. XII,
  pp. 509-512, January 1941.

Philosophy in the Poetry of Edwin Arlington Robinson,
  by Estelle Kaplan

PHILOSOPHY IN THE POETRY OF EDWIN ARLINGTON ROBINSON, by
  Elizabeth Nitchie. *Modern Language Notes* (Baltimore), Vol. LVI,
  pp. 317-318, April 1941.
A POET'S PHILOSOPHY, by G[arland] G[reever]. *The Personalist*
  (Los Angeles), Vol. XXII, pp. 219-220, April, Spring 1941.

Edwin Arlington Robinson and His Manuscripts, by Esther Willard Bates

EDWIN ARLINGTTON ROBINSON AND HIS MANUSCRIPTS, by Milton
Ellis. *The New England Quarterly* (Brunswick, Maine), Vol.
XVII, pp. 323-324, June 1944.

EDWIN ARLINGTON ROBINSON AND HIS MANUSCRIPTS, by Denham
Sutcliffe, *Colby Library Quarterly* (Waterville, Maine), Series I,
pp. 131-133, October 1944.

ROBINSON IN FOCUS, by Winfield Townley Scott. *Poetry* (Chicago),
Vol. LXV, pp. 209-214, January 1945.

EDWIN ARLINGTON ROBINSON AND HIS MANUSCRIPTS, by Louise
Dauner. *Modern Language Quarterly* (Seattle), Vol. VI,
pp. 361-362, September 1945.

Edwin Arlington Robinson, by Yvor Winters

VANITY'S IMPATIENT EAR. *Time* (New York), Vol. XLIX, pp. 96, 98,
January 6, 1947.

ON A NEW ENGLAND LYRE, by John Crowe Ransom. *The New York
Times Book Review* (New York), January 19, 1947, pp. 7, 28.
[See ONE POINT AND ANOTHER, *The New York Times Book
Review* (New York), February 16, 1947, p. 8.]

EDWIN ARLINGTON ROBINSON. *The New Yorker* (New York), Vol.
XX, pp. 98-99, February 8, 1947.

EDWIN ARLINGTON ROBINSON. *The United States Quarterly Booklist*
(Washington), Vol. III, p. 14, March 1947.

EDWIN ARLINGTON ROBINSON, by Milton Wilson. *The Canadian
Forum* (Toronto), Vol. XXVI, p. 286, March 1947.

EDWIN ARLINGTON ROBINSON, by George Snell. *The San Francisco
Chronicle* (San Francisco), April 13, 1947, p. 20.

"GREAT AND AUSTERE POET," by Winfield Townley Scott. *Poetry*
(Chicago), Vol. LXX, pp. 94-98, April 1947. [See PROBLEMS OF
A FAMILY MAN, by Yvor Winters, *Poetry* (Chicago) Vol. LXX,
pp. 285-286, August 1947.]

LIVING POEMS. *The New York Herald Tribune Books* (New York),
May 11, 1947, p. 35.

100

Edwin Arlington Robinson, by Louise Dauner, *American Literature*
(Durham, North Carolina), Vol. XIX, pp. 189-191, May 1947.

Edwin Arlington Robinson, by Robert Bunker. *The New Mexico
Quarterly* (Albuquerque), Vol. XVII, pp. 382-383, Autumn 1947.

Edwin Arlington Robinson, by Louise Dauner. *The New England
Quarterly* (Brunswick, Maine), Vol. XX, pp. 427-429,
September 1947.

Edwin Arlington Robinson, by Charles J. Quirk. *Thought* (New
York), Vol. XXIII, pp. 729-730, December 1948.

Untriangulated Stars

The Intimate Robinson, by Emery Neff. *The Nation* (New York),
Vol. CLXV, pp. 506-507, November 8, 1947.

A Poet to His Friend, by George F. Whicher. *The New York Herald
Tribune Books* (New York), January 11, 1948, p. 4.

Untriangulated Stars, by H. L. Varley. *The Springfield Republican*
(Springfield, Massachusetts), January 25, 1948.

A Poet's Honest Self-Appraisal, by Horace Gregory. *The New
York Times Book Review* (New York), February 8, 1948,
pp. 1, 24.

Untriangulated Stars. *The Times Literary Supplement* (London),
No. 2403, p. 111, February 21, 1948.

Poet in America. *Time* (New York), Vol. LI, pp. 110, 112, March
8, 1948.

Untriangulated Stars. *The United States Quarterly Booklist*
(Washington), Vol. IV, p. 39, March 1948.

Untriangulated Stars, by Louise Dauner. *American Literature*
(Durham, North Carolina), Vol. XX, pp. 78-80, March 1948.

Untriangulated Stars, by Louise Dauner. *The New England
Quarterly* (Brunswick, Maine), Vol. XXI, pp. 111-114, March
1948.

Untriangulated Stars. *Wisconsin Library Bulletin* (Madison),
Vol. XLIV, p. 82. April 1948.

Untriangulated Stars, by Theodore Maynard. *The Catholic World*
(New York), Vol. CLXVIII, p. 87, October 1948.

Edwin Arlington Robinson, by Emery Neff

E. A. ROBINSON—A NEW STUDY, by Robert Davis Gorham. *The New York Times Book Review* (New York), October 24, 1948, pp. 14, 16.

"EAT ROCKS," by William Carlos Williams. *The Nation* (New York), Vol. CLXVII, pp. 498-499, October 30, 1948.

CREATORS OF "WALDEN" AND "TRISTRAM," by Milton Crane. *The Saturday Review of Literature* (New York), Vol. XXI, pp. 12-13, November 13, 1948.

EDWIN ARLINGTON ROBINSON, by J. Z. *More Books: The Bulletin of the Boston Public Library* (Boston), Vol. XXIII, pp. 387-388, December 1948.

EDWIN ARLINGTON ROBINSON, by Louise Dauner. *The New England Quarterly* (Brunswick, Maine), Vol. XXII, pp. 111-113, March 1949.

EDWIN ARLINGTON ROBINSON, by Lewis Leary. *The South Atlantic Quarterly* (Durham, North Carolina), Vol. XLVIII, pp. 617-618, October 1949.

EDWIN ARLINGTON ROBINSON, by John B. Harcourt. *American Quarterly* (Philadelphia), Vol. III, pp. 81-87 [82-83], Spring 1951.

EDWIN ARLINGTON ROBINSON, by Herman E. Spivey. *American Litererature* (Durham, North Carolint), Vol. XXIV, pp. 258-261, May 1952.

The Library of Edwin Arlington Robinson,
  by James Humphry, III

THE LIBRARY OF EDWIN ARLINGTON ROBINSON, by William White. *The Papers of the Bibliographical Society of America* (New York), Vol. XLV, pp. 185-186, Second Quarter 1951.

THE LIBRARY OF EDWIN ARLINGTON ROBINSON, by Denham Sutcliffe. *The New England Quarterly* (Brunswick, Maine), Vol. XXIV, pp. 270-271, June 1951.

Edwin Arlington Robinson, by Ellsworth Barnard

EDWIN ARLINGTON ROBINSON. *Bulletin from Virginia Kirkus'
Bookshop Service* (New York), Vol. XIX, p. 721, December 15,
1951.

OUT OF ONE CENTURY HE SPOKE TO ANOTHER, by Horace Gregory.
The New York Times Book Review (New York), February
10, 1952, p. 18.

AMERICAN POET. *Time* (New York), Vol. LIX, pp. 100, 102, February
11, 1952.

EDWIN ARLINGTON ROBINSON, by G. D. McDonald. *Library Journal*
(New York), Vol. LXXVII, p. 358, February 15, 1952.

PERSPECTIVES ON A POET, by W[infield] T[ownley] Scott. *The
Saturday Review* (New York), Vol. XXXV, p. 13, March 15,
1952.

EDWIN ARLINGTON ROBINSON, by Richard Sullivan. *The Chicago
Tribune* (Chicago), June 29, 1952, p. 12.

EDWIN ARLINGTON ROBINSON. *The United States Quarterly Booklist*
(Washington), Vol. VIII, p. 131, June 1952.

EDWIN ARLINGTON ROBINSON, by Katherine Brégy. *The Catholic
World* (New York), Vol. CLXXV, p. 319, July 1952.

EDWIN ARLINGTON ROBINSON, by Helen Bevington. *The South Atlantic
Quarterly* (Durham, North Carolina), Vol. LI, p. 468, July 1952.

EDWIN ARLINGTON ROBINSON, by Carlyle King. *The Canadian Forum*
(Toronto), Vol. XXXII, p. 119, August 1952.

ROBINSON'S POETRY, by Edwin S. Fussell. *The Kenyon Review*
(Gambier, Ohio), Vol. XIV, pp. 694-697, Autumn
1952.

MR. BARNARD'S ROBINSON: C+, by Louis O. Coxe. *Poetry* (Chicago),
Vol. LXXXI, pp. 187-191, December 1952.

EDWIN ARLINGTON ROBINSON, by Charles Child Walcutt. *The Arizona
Quarterly* (Tucson), Vol. IX, pp. 84-85, Spring 1953.

EDWIN ARLINGTON ROBINSON, by W[illiam] H. D[avenport]. *The
Personalist* (Los Angeles), Vol. XXXIV, p. 206, April, Spring
1953.

Edwin Arlington Robinson, by Edwin S. Fussell

TRADITIONAL POET, by W[infield] T[ownley] S[cott]. *The Saturday Review* (New York), Vol. XXXVII, p. 39, November 20, 1954.

EDWIN ARLINGTON ROBINSON. *The United States Quarterly Booklist* (Washington), Vol. X, p. 500, December 1954.

EDWIN ARLINGTON ROBINSON, by Robert H. Sproat. *Quarterly Journal of Speech* (Bloomington, Indiana), Vol. XLI, p. 204, April 1955.

EDWIN ARLINGTON ROBINSON, by C[harles] Cestre. *Études Anglaises* (Paris), Vol. VIII, p. 181, Avril-Juin 1955.

A TRADITIONAL POET. *The Times Literary Supplement* (London), No. 2794, p. 539, September 16, 1955.

EDWIN ARLINGTON ROBINSON, by Richard Crowder. *Modern Language Notes* (Baltimore), Vol. LXX, pp. 537-539, November 1955.

EDWIN ARLINGTON ROBINSON, by Robert H. Elias. *American Literature* (Durham, North Carolina), Vol. XXVII, pp. 437-438, November 1955.

AN ESSAY ON ROBINSON'S READING, by Denham Sutcliffe. *The Kenyon Review* (Gambier, Ohio), Vol. XVII, pp. 136-139, Winter 1955.

GLOW-WORMS AND ANTIMACASSARS, by Hugh Kenner. *Poetry* (Chicago), Vol. XCII, pp. 121-126 [122-123], May 1958.

Selected Early Poems and Letters

OLD VOICES AND NEW, by August Derleth. *Voices: A Journal of Poetry* (Portland, Maine), No. 177, p. 62, January-April 1962.

Selected Poems

SELECTED POEMS. *The Booklist* (Middletown, Connecticut), Vol. LXII, p. 392, December 15, 1965.

SELECTED POEMS. *The Virginia Quarterly Review* (Charlottesville, Virginia), Vol. XLII, p. xviii, Winter 1966.

CHARACTER IN VERSE, by Edward Pell. *The New Leader* (New York), Vol. XLIX, pp. 29-30, January 17, 1966.

SELECTED POEMS. *American Literature* (Durham, North Carolina), Vol. XXXVII, p. 521, January 1966.

OTHER VOICES, OTHER RHYTHMS, by Robert D. Spector. *The Saturday Review* (New York), Vol. XLIX, pp. 42-44, February 19, 1966.

HE SURVIVES HIS POPULARITY, by Philip Booth. *The Christian Science Monitor* (Boston), Vol. LVIII, p. 7, February 24, 1966.

SELECTED POEMS, by George Brandon Saul. *College English* (Chicago), Vol. XXVII, p. 517, March 1966.

"THERE YET REMAINS WHAT FASHION CANNOT KILL," by William Stafford. *Poetry* (Chicago), Vol. CVIII, pp. 187-188, June 1966.

Where the Light Falls, by Chard Powers Smith

WHERE THE LIGHT FALLS, by Lloyd W. Griffin. *Library Journal* (New York), Vol. XC, p. 1706, April 1, 1965.

POET OF THE RECENT PAST, by Granville Hicks. *The Saturday Review* (New York), Vol. XLVIII, pp. 31-32, April 10, 1965.

WHERE THE LIGHT FALLS, *The Virginia Quarterly Review* (Charlottesville, Virginia), Vol. XLI, p.xc, Summer 1965.

LANCELOT "RODE ON ALONE," by Joel Porte. *The Christian Science Monitor* (Boston), Vol. LVII, p. 7, July 8, 1965.

WHO WAS THE POET'S GUINEVERE?, by Winfield Townley Scott. *The New York Times Book Review* (New York), Vol. LXX, p. 4, September 5, 1965.

WHERE THE LIGHT FALLS. *Choice* (Middletown, Connecticut), Vol. II, p. 390, September 1965.

WHERE THE LIGHT FALLS, by Ellsworth Barnard. *American Literature* (Durham, North Carolina), Vol. XXXVII, pp. 497-498, January 1966.

ROBINSON AND STEVENS: SOME TANGENTIAL BEARINGS, by George Lensing. *Southern Review* (Baton Rouge, Louisiana), Vol. III, pp. 505-513, Spring 1967.

Edwin Arlington Robinson: A Critical Introduction, by Wallace L. Anderson

EDWIN ARLINGTON ROBINSON: A CRITICAL INTRODUCTION. *American Literature* (Durham, North Carolina), Vol. XXXIX, p. 591, January 1968.

EDWIN ARLINGTON ROBINSON: A CRITICAL INTRODUCTION. *Choice* (Middletown, Connecticut), Vol. V, p. 480, June 1968.

EDWIN ARLINGTON ROBINSON: A CRITICAL INTRODUCTION, by Floyd Stovall. *American Literature* (Durham, North Carolina), Vol. XLI, pp. 294-295, May 1969.

EDWIN ARLINGTON ROBINSON: A CRITICAL INTRODUCTION, by Philip R. Yannella. *Modern Language Journal* (Milwaukee, Wisconsin), Vol. LIV, p. 293, April 1970.

Edwin Arlington Robinson: A Poetry of the Act, by W. R. Robinson

EDWIN ARLINGTON ROBINSON: A POETRY OF THE ACT. *The Virginia Quarterly Review* (Charlottesville, Virginia), Vol. XLIV, p. xxiii, Winter 1968.

EDWIN ARLINGTON ROBINSON: A POETRY OF THE ACT, by Ellsworth Barnard. *American Literature* (Durham, North Carolina), Vol. XL, pp. 244-245, May 1968.

EDWIN ARLINGTON ROBINSON: A POETRY OF THE ACT. *Choice* (Middletown, Connecticut), Vol. V, p. 779, September 1968.

EDWIN ARLINGTON ROBINSON: A POETRY OF THE ACT, by Charles T. Davis. *English Language Notes* (Boulder, Colorado), Vol. VI, pp. 226-228, March 1969.

Letters to Edith Brower

EDWIN ARLINGTON ROBINSON'S LETTERS TO EDITH BROWER. *Publishers' Weekly* (New York), Vol. CXCIV, pp. 48-49, July 1, 1968.

ROBINSON LETTERS ARE PUBLISHED. *The Boothbay Register* (Boothbay, Maine), August 29, 1968, p. 1.

SILENT APPROVAL, by H[erbert] A. K[enny]. *The Sunday Globe* (Boston), Vol. CXCIV, p. 46-A, September 8, 1968.

HARVARD PRESS PUBLISHES BOOK OF ROBINSON. *The Morning Sentinel* (Waterville, Maine), October 4, 1968, p. 7.

EDWIN ARLINGTON ROBINSON'S LETTERS TO EDITH BROWER, by Marjorie R. Kohn. *Library Journal* (New York), Vol. XCIII, p. 3788, October 15, 1968.

EDWIN ARLINGTON ROBINSON'S LETTERS TO EDITH BROWER, by David
    E. Philips. *Down East* (Camden, Maine), Vol. XV, p. 66,
    November 1968.
ROBINSON, EDWIN ARLINGTON. *The Booklist* (Chicago), Vol. LXV,
    p. 344, November 15, 1968.
EDWIN ARLINGTON ROBINSON'S LETTERS TO EDITH BROWER.
    The Virginia Quarterly Review (Charlottesville, Virginia),
    Vol. XLV, p. xxx, Winter 1969.
EDWIN ARLINGTON ROBINSON'S LETTERS TO EDITH BROWER. *American
    Literature* (Durham, North Carolina), Vol. XL, p. 594, January
    1969.
THE POET AS CRITIC, by Harry Hayden Clark. *The CEA Critic*
    (Newark, New Jersey), Vol. III, p. 3, February 1969.
THREE LITERARY GIANTS, by William White. *The American Book
    Collector* (Chicago), Vol. XIX, p. 4, April-May 1969.
EDWIN ARLINGTON ROBINSON'S LETTERS TO EDITH BROWER, by Louis
    Budd. *The South Atlantic Quarterly* (Durham, North Carolina),
    Vol. LXVIII, pp. 430-431, Summer 1969.
EDWIN ARLINGTON ROBINSON'S LETTERS TO EDITH BROWER,
    by Paschal Reeves, *Georgia Review* (Athens, Georgia),
    Vol. XXIV, pp. 238-239, Summer 1970.

Edwin Arlington Robinson,
   by Hoyt C. Franchere

EDWIN ARLINGTON ROBINSON, by Charles T. Davis. *American
    Literature* (Durham, North Carolina), Vol. XLII, pp. 588-590,
    January 1971.

Edwin Arlington Robinson: The Life of Poetry,
   by Louis O. Coxe

POET OF LONER, LOSER, ANTIHERO, OUTSIDER, by Victor Howes. *The
    Christian Science Monitor* (Boston), Vol. LXI, p. 9, March 15,
    1969.
THE POET OF SECRET LIVES AND MISSPENT OPPORTUNITIES, by James
    Dickey. *The New York Times Book Review* (New York), Vol.
    LXXIV, pp. 1, 10, May 18, 1969.

A BAGPIPE IN A MADHOUSE, by Jerrold Hickey. *The Sunday Globe*
(Boston), Vol. 195, p. B-37, June 22, 1969.
EDWIN ARLINGTON ROBINSON: THE LIFE OF POETRY, by Charles T.
Davis. *American Literature* (Durham, North Carolina), Vol. XLII,
pp. 588-590, January 1971.

Appreciation of Edwin Arlington Robinson,
edited by Richard Cary

COLBY VOLUME HONORS POET E. A. ROBINSON. *The Morning Sentinel*
(Waterville, Maine), December 15, 1969, p. 6.
APPRECIATION OF EDWIN ARLINGTON ROBINSON, by Geoffrey Elan.
Yankee (Dublin, New Hampshire), Vol. XXXIV, p. 175,
February 1970.
APPRECIATION OF EDWIN ARLINGTON ROBINSON, by David E. Philips.
Down East (Camden, Maine), Vol. XVI, p. 88, April 1970.
APPRECIATION OF EDWIN ARLINGTON ROBINSON, by Walter Waring.
Library Journal (New York), Vol. XCV, pp. 1743-1744, May
1, 1970.
APPRECIATION OF EDWIN ARLINGTON ROBINSON. *American Literature*
(Durham, North Carolina), Vol. XLII, p. 271, May 1970.

Edwin Arlington Robinson: A Collection of Critical Essays,
edited by Francis Murphy

EDWIN ARLINGTON ROBINSON: A COLLECTION OF CRITICAL ESSAYS,
by Walter W. Waring. *Library Journal* (New York), Vol.
XCV, p. 2480, July 1970.

Edwin Arlington Robinson: Centenary Essays
edited by Ellsworth Barnard

ESSAYS ON POET ROBINSON COVER A WIDE SPECTRUM OF OPINIONS,
by Louis Coxe. *The Boston Globe* (Boston), January 26, 1970,
p. 13.
EDWIN A. ROBINSON: TIME DEALS KINDLY WITH POET, by Glenn
Griffin. *The Atlanta Journal* [and] *Constitution* (Atlanta), March
29, 1970, p. 16-D.

108

AN EARNED TRIBUTE TO A FINE POET, by David Allan Evans. *The Minneapolis Tribune* (Minneapolis), April 12, 1970, p. E-10.

EDWIN ARLINGTON ROBINSON: CENTENARY ESSAYS. *American Literature* (Durham, North Carolina), Vol. XLII, p. 426, November 1970.

EDWIN ARLINGTON ROBINSON: CENTENARY ESSAYS, by John T. Flanagan. *The South Atlantic Quarterly* (Durham, North Carolina), Vol. LXX, pp. 129-130, Winter 1971.

D. Theses

Note.—Unless otherwise noted, the following M.A. and Ph.D. theses, wholly on Robinson or largely so, are unpublished; those issued in book form are so designated, with reference to the section on *Books* above, and for those abstracted in *Dissertation Abstracts* readers are referred to the section on *Periodicals*.

1918

EDWIN ARLINGTON ROBINSON, by Clytie Hazel Kearney. New York: Columbia University.

1925

EDWIN ARLINGTON ROBINSON: A BIOGRAPHICAL AND CRITICAL STUDY, by Beulah B. Clark. Columbus: Ohio State University.

EDWIN ARLINGTON ROBINSON'S STRUGGLE AGAINST PURITANISM, by Catherine Elizabeth Holman. Norman: University of Oklahoma.

1926

TWO ASPECTS OF THE POETRY OF EDWIN ARLINGTON ROBINSON, by W. H. Johnson, Jr. Nashville, Tennessee: Vanderbilt University. 82 pp.

ARTHURIAN STORY RETOLD BY EDWIN ARLINGTON ROBINSON, by Ruth N. Lechlitner. Iowa City: State University of Iowa.

1927

POEMS OF EDWIN ARLINGTON ROBINSON, by Justin J. Doyle. Rochester, New York: University of Rochester. (Hull Prize Essay.)

A STUDY OF THE TREATMENT OF SOME ARTHURIAN MATERIAL BY TENNYSON AND ROBINSON, by Dora May Hill. Chicago: University of Chicago. 82 pp.

PHILOSOPHY OF LIGHT: AN ESSAY ON THE POETRY OF EDWIN
ARLINGTON ROBINSON, by Ronald W. P. King. Rochester,
New York: University of Rochester. (Hull Prize Essay.)
THE POETRY OF EDWIN ARLINGTON ROBINSON, by Ruth E. Latta.
Rochester, New York: University of Rochester. (William
Memorial Prize Essay.)

1928

AN ANALYSIS OF THE EPIC POETRY OF JOHN GNEISENAN NEIHARDT,
ALFRED NOYES, AND EDWIN ARLINGTON ROBINSON WITH
RESPECT TO THE IMMORTAL LINE, by Anna Catherine Burtless.
Lincoln: University of Nebraska.
THE TRISTRAM STORY IN EDWIN ARLINGTON ROBINSON'S TRISTRAM,
by Claude Hansen Christensen. Chicago: University of Chicago.
97 pp.
THREE RECENT TRISTRAMS: A COMPARISON OF THE VERSIONS BY
THOMAS HARDY, EDWIN ARLINGTON ROBINSON, AND JOHN
MASEFIELD, by Harold O. Grauel. Columbus: Ohio State
University.
ROBINSON AND THE ARTHURIAN LEGEND, by Puryear Mims. Nashville,
Tennessee: Vanderbilt University. 75 pp.

1929

THE TECHNIQUE OF EDWIN ARLINGTON ROBINSON AND ROBERT
FROST, by Louise Knutson Altman. Seattle: University of
Washington.
THE DRAMATIC ELEMENTS IN THE NEW ENGLAND CHARACTERIZA-
TIONS OF FROST, ROBINSON, AND AMY LOWELL, by Martha
Frances Beede. Columbus: Ohio State University.
EDWIN ARLINGTON ROBINSON—A CRITICAL ESTIMATE OF HIS POETRY,
by Thomas Carroll Hefferman. Chestnut Hill: Boston College.
A COMPARATIVE STUDY OF THE TRISTRAM STORY OF THE OLD ENGLISH
LEGEND AS IT IS TOLD IN MODERN POETRY BY MATTHEW
ARNOLD, ALGERNON CHARLES SWINBURNE, AND EDWIN
ARLINGTON ROBINSON, by Marcella Reidy. Albuquerque:
University of New Mexico.

1930

THE METRICS AND IMAGERY OF EDWIN ARLINGTON ROBINSON,
AS EXHIBITED IN FIVE OF HIS BLANK VERSE POEMS, by Mrs. Elsie
Ruth (Dykes) Chant. Albuquerque: University of New Mexico.

THE POETRY OF EDWIN ARLINGTON ROBINSON, by Martha Peace
Knight. Ithaca: Cornell University.

1931

THE LEGEND OF TRISTRAM IN THE WORKS OF HARDY, MASEFIELD
AND ROBINSON, by Nelle Viola Brannon. Lincoln: University
of Nebraska.

COMPARATIVE ANALYSIS OF THE TRISTRAM OF MASEFIELD AND
ROBINSON WITH HISTORICAL BACKGROUND, by Hoyt Catlin
Franchere. Iowa City: State University of Iowa.

INFLUENCES ON EDWIN ARLINGTON ROBINSON, by Laura C. Johnston.
Bronx, New York: Fordham University.

EDWIN ARLINGTON ROBINSON'S TREATMENT OF ARTHURIAN LEGENDS,
by Lola Rivers Thompson. Austin: University of Texas.

1932

A CRITIQUE OF E. A. ROBINSON'S USE OF THE TRISTRAM LEGEND
WITH REFERENCE TO BEDIER AND MALORY AND TO THE REST OF
ROBINSON'S WORKS, by Dorothy Bonawit. New York:
Columbia University.

STUDY OF SOME PHASES OF THE POETRY OF EDWIN ARLINGTON
ROBINSON, by Sister Mary Mauritius Duffy. Iowa City:
State University of Iowa.

ATTITUDES OF EDWIN ARLINGTON ROBINSON AND CERTAIN SIMILAR
IDEAS EXPRESSED IN HIS POETRY AND THE POETRY OF ROBERT
BROWNING, by Bess Raisel Dworsky. Minneapolis: University
of Minnesota.

POETIC TECHNIQUE IN THE VERSE OF MILLAY, ROBINSON JEFFERS,
AND EDWIN ARLINGTON ROBINSON, by Robert Norris Hughes.
Columbus: Ohio State University.

THE METRICS, IMAGERY, AND PHILOSOPHY OF EDWIN ARLINGTON
ROBINSON AS SHOWN IN HIS NON-BLANK VERSE POETRY,
by Nell Snyder Rhoades. Albuquerque: New Mexico University.

1933

ARTHURIAN POEMS OF EDWIN ARLINGTON ROBINSON, by Varnelle
Braddy. Atlanta: Emory University.

A STUDY OF THE WOMEN CHARACTERS IN THE POETRY OF EDWIN
ARLINGTON ROBINSON, by Jessie Harold. Lawrence:
University of Kansas.

METAPHYSICAL ASPECTS OF AMERICAN POETRY, by Mildred Dodge
Ingalls. Medford, Massachusetts: Tufts College.

THE METRICS AND IMAGERY OF EDWIN ARLINGTON ROBINSON AS
EXHIBITED IN SIXTEEN OF HIS BLANK VERSE POEMS, by Louise
Rucker Wells. Albuquerque: University of New Mexico.

1934

A STUDY OF THE POET AS AGNOSTIC, WITH REFERENCE TO MATTHEW
ARNOLD, CONRAD AIKEN, ROBINSON JEFFERS, THOMAS STEARNS
ELIOT, EDWIN ARLINGTON ROBINSON, by Frances Eldredge.
Medford, Massachusetts: Tufts College.

CHARACTER PORTRAYAL IN THE WORK OF EDWIN ARLINGTON
ROBINSON, by Dorothy Margaret Latchem. Iowa City: State
University of Iowa.

1935

ARTHURIAN MATERIAL IN AMERICAN LITERATURE, by Dorothy Hughes.
Lincoln: University of Nebraska.

1936

EDWIN ARLINGTON ROBINSONS LANGERE VERSERZAHLUNGEN,
by Elisabeth Grohs. Vienna: University of Vienna.

1940

PHILOSOPHY IN THE POETRY OF EDWIN ARLINGTON ROBINSON,
   by Estelle Kaplan. New York: Columbia University. [See *Books*,
   1940, above.]

1943

SOME ASPECTS OF THE PHILOSOPHY OF EDWIN ARLINGTON ROBINSON:
   SELF-KNOWLEDGE, SELF-ACCEPTANCE, AND CONSCIENCE,
   by Seymour Betsky. Cambridge: Harvard University.
   [See *Periodicals*, 1945, above.]

1944

THREE STUDIES OF EDWIN ARLINGTON ROBINSON: HIS MALE
   CHARACTERS, HIS EMERGENCE, AND HIS CONTEMPORANEOUS
   REPUTATION, by Richard H. Crowder. Iowa City: State University
   of Iowa. [See *Periodicals*, 1945, above.]
STUDIES IN EDWIN ARLINGTON ROBINSON, by Margaret L[ouise]
   Dauner. Iowa City: State University of Iowa. [See *Periodicals*,
   1944, above.]

1948

EDWIN ARLINGTON ROBINSON AND THE ARTHURIAN LEGEND,
   by Laurence D. Perrine. New Haven: Yale University.

1949

THE EARLY POETRY OF EDWIN ARLINGTON ROBINSON, by Edwin S.
   Fussell. Cambridge: Harvard University. [See *Books*, 1954, above.]
A CRITICAL ACCOUNT OF THE WORK OF ROBINSON IN THE LIGHT OF
   ITS POSITION IN AMERICAN THOUGHT AND AMERICAN LITERARY
   HISTORY, by Dwight L. Durling. Flushing, New York:
   Queens College.
ROBINSON'S SONNETS, by George Mitchell. Philadelphia: Temple
   University.

1951

THE POETIC DRAMA OF MOODY, ROBINSON, TORRENCE, AND
MACKAYE, 1894-1909, by Charles T. Davis. New York:
New York University.

1952

DAS LYRISCHE WERK EDWIN ARLINGTON ROBINSON, by Alfred
Baumgärtner. Mainz: Mainz University.

1953

CHRISTIAN CONSERVATISM IN THE POETRY OF EDWIN ARLINGTON
ROBINSON, by David H. Burton. Washington: Georgetown
University.

1954

THE SHORTER NARRATIVE POEMS OF EDWIN ARLINGTON ROBINSON,
by Alan Archer Stephens, Jr. Columbia: University of Missouri.

1955

EDWIN ARLINGTON ROBINSON AND ALANSON TUCKER SCHUMANN:
A STUDY IN INFLUENCES, by Peter Dechert. Philadelphia:
University of Pennsylvania. 225 pp. [See *Periodicals*, 1955, above.]
EDWIN ARLINGTON ROBINSON AS DRAMATIST AND DRAMATIC POET,
by Lucy Dickinson Fryxell. Lexington: University of Kentucky.
161 pp. [See *Periodicals*, 1960, above.]

1956

E. A. ROBINSON'S PRINCIPLES AND PRACTICE OF HIS POETRY:
THE EFFECTS OF HIS PRINCIPLES OF POETRY ON THE TECHNIQUE
AND STRUCTURE OF THE POEMS, by Robert David Stevick.
Madison: University of Wisconsin. 305 pp. [See *Periodicals*,
1956, above.]
ORGANIC FORM IN THE SHORTER POEMS OF EDWIN ARLINGTON
ROBINSON, by Elmer Samuel Moon. Ann Arbor: University of
Michigan. 283 pp. [See *Periodicals*, 1957, above.]

PSYCHOLOGICAL ASPECTS OF THE POETRY OF EDWIN ARLINGTON
ROBINSON, by Paul Hampton Morrill. Evanston, Illinois:
Northwestern University. 189 pp. [See *Periodicals*, 1957, above.]

1961

CHARACTER AND STRUCTURE IN EDWIN ARLINGTON ROBINSON'S
MAJOR NARRATIVES, by John Vail Foy. Ithaca: Cornell University.
268 pp. [See *Periodicals*, 1961, above.]

1962

THE ENGAGING MASK: ISOLATION IN THE EARLY POEMS OF EDWIN
ARLINGTON ROBINSON, by Joseph Fetler Malof. Los Angeles:
University of California. [See *Periodicals*, 1962, above.]
EDWIN ARLINGTON ROBINSON: THE POETRY OF THE ACT, by William
Ronald Robinson. Columbus: Ohio State University, 239 pp.
[See *Periodicals*, 1963, and *Books*, 1967, above.]

1965

THE HAPPY ENDING AS A CONTROLLING COMIC ELEMENT IN THE
POETIC PHILOSOPHY OF EDWIN ARLINGTON ROBINSON,
by Sara Louise Mott. Columbia: University of South Carolina.
183 pp. [See *Periodicals*, 1966, above.]
THE SHORTER POEMS OF THOMAS HARDY AND EDWIN ARLINGTON
ROBINSON: A STUDY IN CONTRASTS, by Paul Nathan Zietlow.
Ann Arbor: University of Michigan, 224 pp. [See *Periodicals*,
1965, above.]

1966

ROBINSON AND THE BIBLE, by Nicholas Ayo. Durham, North Carolina:
Duke University. 251 pp. [See *Periodicals*, 1966, above.]
MERLIN, LANCELOT, AND TRISTRAM: E. A. ROBINSON'S ARTHURIAN
POEMS ON MAN'S DILEMMA, by Patricia O'Donnell Ewers.
Chicago: Loyola University.

EDWIN ARLINGTON ROBINSON'S VIEW OF POETRY: A STUDY OF HIS
THEORY AND HIS TECHNIQUES IN THE LATE NARRATIVES,
by Nancy Carol Joyner. Chapel Hill: The University of North
Carolina. 247 pp. [See *Periodicals*, 1967, above.]

WITH FIRM ADDRESS: A CRITICAL STUDY OF 26 SHORTER POEMS
OF E. A. ROBINSON, by Ronald Wesson Moran. Baton Rouge:
Louisiana State University. 201 pp. [See *Periodicals*, 1966, above.]

1967

THE SOURCES OF THE IMAGERY IN THE POETRY OF E. A. ROBINSON,
by Elise Dort Isely. Fayetteville: University of Arkansas.
189 pp. [See *Periodicals*, 1967, above.]

NARRATIVE FORM IN THE LONG POEMS OF EDWIN ARLINGTON
ROBINSON, by Richard Samuel Moseley, III. Cincinnati: University
of Cincinnati. 282 pp. [See *Periodicals*, 1968, above.]

1968

SOME PURITAN CHARACTERISTICS OF THE POETRY OF EDWIN
ARLINGTON ROBINSON, by James Anthony Gowen. Stanford
University, California: Stanford University. 216 pp.
[See *Periodicals*, 1968, above.]

THE *MAKARIS* OF CAMELOT, by Celia B. Morris. New York: The
City University of New York. 360 pp. [See *Periodicals*,
1968, above.]

1969

EDWIN ARLINGTON ROBINSON AS SOCIAL CRITIC AND MORAL GUIDE,
by John Cashion Bierk. Evanston, Illinois: Northwestern
University. 211 pp. [See *Periodicals*, 1970, above.]

MAJOR CATEGORIES OF IRONY IN THE POETRY OF EDWIN ARLINGTON
ROBINSON, by Leon James Satterfield. Lincoln: The University
of Nebraska. 195 pp. [See *Periodicals*, 1970, above.]

Part V. Writings Hitherto Uncollected

Note.—With the cooperation of Professor Richard Cary, of Colby College, and the permission of Mrs. Harold Holt, Gardiner, Maine, and Professor David S. Nivison, of Stanford University, the following few pieces of Robinson's uncollected poetry and prose are included for the convenience of collectors and scholars. All of the material has been previously published and is reprinted exactly as in the original appearance. I have not, as Mr. Hogan did in his *Bibliography*, reprinted letters and excerpts from letters, nor the notes to the poet's nieces, because Professor Wallace L. Anderson, of the University of Northern Iowa, has been for some time preparing a multivolume edition of EAR's letters, to be published by Harvard University Press.

Although I have listed above in Part III "[Three Articles]" by Robinson, "The Next 'Great Poet,'" "Incompetent and Capable Novelists," and "Commercial Potency and Literary Significance," reprinted in *The Colby Mercury* in 1941, I am not reprinting them here. On the basis of evidence presented by Alice Meacham Williams, "Edwin Arlington Robinson, Journalist," *The New England Quarterly*, Vol. XV, pp. 715-724, December 1942, I agree with her conclusion that they are not by Robinson. Everything else below is unquestionably by EAR. Mr. Hogan's note to "Bores," in Part III, above, is certainly convincing; "Isaac Pitman" is signed by Robinson; Mrs. Williams, in the article just cited, proves that Robinson wrote "The Balm of Custom"; and for the others, Robinson gave permission during his lifetime, or the editors or authors of the original printings may be consulted for their ascription of them to the poet.—W. W.

BORES

Looking back into the dark ages, when the stake and block nearly ruled the world, when a man was put to the rack for some trivial offence, which at the present day would hardly attract notice, and multitudes were burned at the stake for some religious difference, and then turning to the present, we marvel at the change.

The advancing centuries brought with them a civilization which pictured before the people the deeds of former days; the tortures were gradually abandoned, and people slowly gained their rights. Their deeds no longer appeared as just punishment of crime, but as a dark blot on progress, justice and civilization.

Man's duty on this earth is the performance of that which will benefit not only himself, but the community. He should work for his own interest, but at the same time for the public good; he should learn and act accordingly; he should obey the laws and live peaceably; he should mind his own business.

This is what he should do: Travel over the country, or read the daily papers and histories, and see what he does; visit the slums and narrow alleys of our great cities, and draw his own conclusions at the signs of degradation on every hand.

"There among the glooming alleys, progress halts with palsied foot."

No nation can progress as rapidly when continually harrassed by events which butt against the walls of justice; no individual can succeed as well when constantly held back by some outside matter. If we can imagine the state of the nation fifty years hence, enlightened by fifty years of experiment and study, could we imagine it free from obstacles, which in themselves amount to nothing, but by their numbers assume the form of a snag, blocking the paths of civilization?

In every city, town and village (this city not excepted), there is always to be found a brigade whose food consists of other people's affairs, who are always ready to predict marriages for months ahead, who can always find some fault with another's new bonnet, who delight in sending out a corps of urchins after votes, providing the place is large enough to hold a fair.

Even in country villages people sometimes die, and then there is a funeral. Does it not seem a sufficient trial to bear the loss of a friend, without being compelled to listen to a three or four hours' harangue by a preacher who reviews everything, from the fall of Adam to the Cambridge strike, and supposes he is teaching some great moral lesson, but at the end is no nearer his point than when he begun? It is truly said, "many a minister is the undertaker of the subject he undertakes."

At the present day the world is overflowing with a light class of literature, much of which in material has the same ideas and ends, usually spun to a tiresome length, and containing page after page of des[c]ription, which is copied almost verbatim into each book the author writes. The excessive perusal of this line of literature blunts the mind of the reader, who in a short time can appreciate no other style. The excessive sale encourages the production, and any one can see the result.

So it may be found in every phase of life. One man takes things as they come, and makes the best of it; another is continually growling, and throws a dark shadow between himself and every one he meets.

Now the entire category of these disciples of Reversion should be bound together by a withe twisted from their own actions, tagged for Astolat, (the crippled servitor once more called out,) and sent "upward with the flood."

The Amateur (Gardiner, Maine), 1887, pp. 10-11.

ISAAC PITMAN

With many a whirling dash of dim design
  He snares the flying thought in frenzy flung;
  The captive cadence of the human tongue
Follows his hand, immured in every line;
His labor through the centuries will shine,
  And when this old man dwells no more among
  The living, where his glories long have rung,
Calling his fellows to the phonic shrine—

120

Still will he walk Fame's flowering avenues,
  Amid rich gardens through his life-work sown—
  Fairer than vineyards in far Sicily;
And here the Master, mutely musing, views
  New flowers springing where the old have grown,
  The princely pageant of posterity.

The Phonographic World (New York),
Vol. V, p. 280, May 1890.

THE BALM OF CUSTOM

There are some thousands of excellent Democrats who will vote for Mr. [William Jennings] Bryan this fall because they have "got used to him." They will not vote for him because they have made a logical analysis—so far as such a thing is possible—of his curiously complicated ethics; they will not vote for him because they believe that Bryanism, as a rejuvenating abstraction, is the one thing that will save this Western world from damnation and eclipse. But they will vote for him, and they will do it because he is no longer an object of unqualified terror to them. They will take him as a matter of course. They will take him somewhat as an uncomplaining farmer would take a blight or a long drouth—as a part of the Great Plan.

It is much easier to vote than it is to think, and it is far more restful to yield to the subtle magnetism of a good old word like Democrat than it is to dedicate a few "sessions of sweet, silent thought" to finding out what the word means as it is used today in the United States of America. No honest man would encourage any illusions in regard to the simplicity of such an undertaking, but one might venture to wish that some of his pacific fellow countrymen would at least put to themselves the question of the immortal Congressman who did not know where he was "at." They are not silver men, they are "not exactly anti-imperialists"; they are just Democrats. They do not show specific symptoms of even the most remote forms of Bryanistic unrest; they do not seem to be more than casually restless over anything. Marjorie Fleming would say that they are more than usually calm. They did not vote for Mr. Bryan in 1896, for he was a novelty then and they were afraid of him; but they will vote for him in 1900, for he is no longer a novelty and they are no longer afraid of him. Custom has so staled his infinite monotony that he does not seem to them to be half so dangerous as he used to be.

They are willing enough to confess that Mr. Bryan has a few peculiar attributes that are not wholly admirable, and some of them will say that they have occasional suggestions of something like doubt as to the alleged infallibility of his prophetic genius. They have heard that he can read the future as well as an ordinary man can read a newspaper, and a few of them may have heard that his persistent association with "things that are to be" has been bad for his sense of proportion, and positively shocking to his realization of the prophetic significance of things that are. But all this need not dishearten them. It is said that Michelangelo, after completing his work on the ceiling of the Sistine Chapel, could not read a book with any comfort without holding it above his head; and if [t]his be true of Michelangelo, what may not be true of Mr. Bryan? If so slight a task as that of painting Biblical allegories on a ceiling may produce such strange results, what may not be the results of trying to decorate the zenith with all sorts of pictorial fables that will not stick? And who is to wonder that Mr. Bryan should be impatient and somewhat irrational? Not these reclaimed and passive supporters of his, assuredly. It is not their duty to wonder; it is their duty to be consistent Democrats. It is just as easy to be consistent as it is to be incredulous.

And therefore they will vote. They will not know precisely what they are voting for, but they will not be annoyed by a little discrepancy like that. They have relaxed themselves into a state of intellectual captivity that has developed [by] degrees into a condition that borders on political Nirvana, and Nirvana is nothing if not painless. Four solid years have been given to them for the attainment of this individual negation, and they appear to have improved every hour of it; they have got used to Mr. Bryan and they are going to do their duty; and they seem to be contented. There is a great deal in getting used to things. The illustrious Lord Byron wrote a famous poem about a man who got so used to being a captive that he regained his freedom with a sigh.

The Daily Tribune (New York), October 7, 1900, p. 8.

[TRIBUTE TO THEODORE ROOSEVELT]

While my personal acquaintance with Colonel [Theodore] Roosevelt may be described as rather slight, his wholly unsuspected appreciation of my work assumed a form that gave me a somewhat unusual acquaintance with certain of his methods, in circumstances that would hardly be familiar to the people at large. It is, therefore, with great pleasure, and with much gratitude, that I record an occurrence which in a life like his may not unlikely have been measured as casual and incidental. But whatever it may have been to him, there was nothing casual or incidental about it so far as I was concerned—especially as it happened at a time when my secular affairs were in a condition that might conservatively have been defined as a little more than precarious and something less than desperate.

But President Roosevelt knew nothing about me or my affairs when a copy of one of my books first found its way into his hands, and for some reason or other not only attracted his fancy, but awoke in him a curiosity as to the sort of being who had written it. Consequently, as I was to learn later, he went promptly out of his official way to write a few letters of inquiry, including one to the late Richard Watson Gilder, then editor of the "Century Magazine," from whom he obtained a former New York address of mine at a time when I was trying to write advertisements in Boston for a man who was of the best, even though his advertisements were not. In addition to transmitting an expired address, Mr. Gilder was able also to give the President a considerable amount of information as to my previous and present condition of servitude, and apparently to encourage him in his belief that my poetry was not altogether deplorable or joyous. There were some strange and reprehensible derelicts in that book of mine; and the stranger and more reprehensible they were, the better the President seemed to like them—probably because they were not fundamentally vicious.

The somewhat prevalent and wholly foolish notion that Colonel Roosevelt was tolerant only, or mainly, of biceps and sunshine was clearly disproved in his disinterested and business-like pursuit of the person who was responsible for this book just mentioned—a book in which the characters, taken together, are of a certainty neither strenuous nor sunny.

They may be interesting, and I hope they are, but I am pretty certain that their combined example would lead one sooner to the devil than to the White House. But as Colonel Roosevelt was manifestly in no danger of going to the devil, and was already in the White House, probably he felt himself to be immune from any contagion of insufficiency and general uselessness to which some of my eccentric citizens may have exposed him. At any rate, he remembered me and finally tracked me to my dingy room in Boston; and in a few days was able to offer me a position in the New York Custom House. And for that attention to a total stranger—an attention that was rewarded, I fear, with varying degrees of diligence and efficiency—I am happy too, owing to Colonel Roosevelt an increasing indebtedness of gratitude for which there is unhappily no tangible return. The best and only acknowledgment that I can make of a most unusual act on the part of a most unusual man must apparently be told only in my gratefulness and in a few inadequate words.

Roosevelt as We Knew Him,
by Frederick S. Wood, 1927, pp. 391-393.

FORTUNATUS

Be as you are; your story is all told,
And all without the cost of augury.
Nothing in years, nothing in chance or fate,
May dent the mail of your complacency.

But as you are, and always as you are;
Grope for no more than may be requisite.
You are among the chosen of the world
Who serve it best when unaware of it.

For while you see it as it never was,
Your ministration will not be in vain;
You will ameliorate the mystery
Somewhat in seeing so little to explain.

124

You will not see the drama of dead lives
That are behind calm faces and closed doors;
You will not feel the weight of heavy chains
That others wear that you may not wear yours;

You will not hear the breathing of the beast
That has been history since there was man;
And seeing not much that need be different,
You will not wonder why it all began.

You will not have to see how small a place
Will be enough to make of you a king;
You will have all there is for you to use,
And having little will have everything.

Reno: The Slide Mountain Press
(J. R. Wells), 1928.

MODRED: A FRAGMENT

Time and the dark
Had come, but not alone. The southern gate
That had been open wide for Lancelot
Made now an entrance for three other men,
Who strode along the gravel or the grass,
Careless of who should hear them. When they came
To the great oak and the two empty chairs,
One paused, and held the others with a tongue
That sang an evil music while it spoke:
"Sit here, my admirable Colgrevance,
And you, my gentle Agravaine, sit here.
For me, well I have had enough of sitting;
And I have heard enough and seen enough
To blast a kingdom into kingdom come,
Had I so fierce a mind—which happily
I have not, for the king here is my father.

There's been a comment and a criticism
Abounding, I believe, in Camelot
For some time at my undeserved expense,
But God forbid that I should make my father
Less happy than he will be when he knows
What I shall have to tell him presently;
And that will only be what he has known
Since Merlin, or the ghost of Merlin, came
Two years ago to warn him. Though he sees,
One thing he will not see; and this must end.
We must have no blind kings in Camelot,
Or we shall have no land worth harrowing,
And our last harvest will be food for strangers.
My father, as you know, has gone a-hunting."

"We know about the king," said Agravaine,
"And you know more than any about the queen.
We are still waiting, Modred. Colgrevance
And I are waiting."

                    Modred laughed at him
Indulgently: "Did I say more than any?
If so, then inadvertently I erred;
For there is one man here, one Lancelot,
Who knows, I fancy, a deal more than I do,
And I know much. Yes, I know more than much.
Yet who shall snuff the light of what he knows
To blind the king he serves? No, Agravaine,
A wick like that would smoke and smell of treason."

"Your words are mostly smoke, if I may say so,"
Said Colgrevance: "What is it you have seen,
And what are we to do? I wish no ill
To Lancelot. I know no evil of him,
Or of the queen; and I'll hear none of either,
Save what you, on your oath, may tell me now.

I look yet for the trail of your dark fancy
To blur your testament."

                "No, Colgrevance,
There are no blurs or fancies exercising
Tonight where I am. Lancelot will ascend
Anon, betimes, and with no drums or shawms
To sound the appointed progress of his feet;
And he will not be lost along the way,
For there are landmarks and he knows them all.
No, Colgrevance, there are no blurs or fancies
Unless it be that your determination
Has made them for your purpose what they seem.
But here I beg your pardon, Colgrevance.
We reticent ones are given to say too much,
With our tongues once in action. Pray forgive.
Your place tonight will be a shadowed alcove,
Where you may see this knight without a stain
While he goes in where no man save the king
Has dared before to follow. Agravaine
And I will meet you on the floor below,
Having already beheld this paragon-Joseph
Go by us for your clinching observation.
Then we, with a dozen or so for strength, will act;
And there shall be no more of Lancelot."

"Modred, I wish no ill to Lancelot,
And I know none of him," said Colgrevance.
"My dream is of a sturdier way than this
For me to serve my king. Give someone else
That alcove, and let me be of the twelve.
I swear it irks the marrow of my soul
To shadow Lancelot—though I may fight him,
If so it is to be. Furthermore, Modred,
You gave me not an inkling of the part
That you have read off now so pleasantly

For me to play. No, Modred, by the God
Who knows the right way and the wrong, I'll be
This night no poisonous inhabitant
Of alcoves in your play, not even for you.
No man were more the vassal of his friend
Than I am, but I'm damned if I'll be owned."

In a becoming darkness Modred smiled
Away the first accession of his anger.
"Say not like that," he answered, musically.
"Be temperate, Colgrevance. Remember always
Your knighthood and your birth. Remember, too,
That I may hold him only as my friend
Who loves me for myself, not for my station.
We're born for what we're born for, Colgrevance;
And you and I and Agravaine are born
To serve our king. It's all for the same end,
Whether we serve in alcoves, or behind
A velvet arras on another floor.
What matters it, if we be loyal men—
With only one defection?"

                    "Which is—what?"
Said Agravaine, who breathed hard and said little,
Albeit he had no fame abroad for silence.

"Delay—procrastination—overcaution—
Or what word now assimilates itself
The best with your inquiring mood, my brother.
These operations that engage us now
Were planned and executed long ago,
Had I but acted then on what was written
No less indelibly than at this hour,
Though maybe not so scorchingly on me.
'If there were only Modred in the way,'—
I heard her saying it—'would you come tonight?'

Saint Brandan! How she nuzzled and smothered him!
Forgive me, Colgrevance, when I say more
Than my raw vanity may reconcile
With afterthought. But that was what she said
To Lancelot, and that was what I heard.
And what I saw was of an even bias
With all she told him here. God, what a woman!
She floats about the court so like a lily,
That even I'd be fooled were I the king,
Seeing with his eyes what I would not see.
But now the stars are crying in their courses
For this to end, and we are men to end it.
Meanwhile, for the king's hunting and his health,
We have tonight a sort of wassailing;
Wherefore we may as well address ourselves,
Against our imminent activities,
To something in the way of trencher service—
Which also is a service to the king.
For they who serve must eat. God save the King!"

They took the way of Lancelot along
The darkened hedges to the palace lights,
With Modred humming lowly to himself
A chant of satisfaction. Colgrevance,
Not healed of an essential injury,
Nor given the will to cancel his new pledge
To Modred, made with neither knowing why,
Passed in without a word, leaving his two
Companions hesitating on the steps
Outside, one scowling and the other smiling.

"Modred, you may have gone an inch too far
With Colgrevance tonight. Why set a trap
For trouble? We've enough with no additions.
His fame is that of one among the faithful,
Without a fear, and fearless without guile."

"And that is why we need him, Agravaine,"
Said Modred, with another singing laugh.
"He'll go as was appointed by his fate
For my necessity. A man to achieve
High deeds must have a Colgrevance or two
Around him for unused emergencies,
And for the daily sweat. Your Colgrevance
May curse himself till he be violet,
Yet he will do your work. There is none else,
Apparently, that God will let him do."

"Not always all of it," said Agravaine.
But Modred answered with another laugh
And led the way in to the wassailing,
Where Dagonet was trolling a new song
To Lancelot, who smiled—as if in pain
To see so many friends and enemies,
All cheering him, all drinking, and all gay.

New York [etc.]: Edmond Byrne Hackett,
The Brick Row Bookshop, Inc., 1929.

THE FIRST SEVEN YEARS

Whenever I have occasion to turn the leaves of a rather formidable looking book of mine entitled *Collected Poems*, the sight of a section of it called *The Children of the Night* is likely to make me realize unwillingly, and with an effort, that some of those early poems were written more than forty years ago. In those days time had no special significance for a certain juvenile and incorrigible fisher of words who thought nothing of fishing for two weeks to catch a stanza, or even a line, that he would not throw back into a squirming sea of language where there was every word but the one he wanted. There were strange and iridescent and impossible words that would seize the bait and swallow the hook and all but drag the excited angler in after them, but like that famous catch of Hiawatha's, they were generally not the fish he wanted. He wanted fish that were smooth and shining and subtle, and very much alive, and not too strange; and presently, after long patience and many rejections, they began to bite.

Many of those slippery victims went into the preparation and final accomplishment of innumerable short poems and sonnets that had certainly many faults and at least one merit. For me, at any rate, there was a sort of merit in their not being quite like anything else—or anything that I remembered. But a kindly providence had given me a modicum of common sense that was always reminding me of my age—from sixteen to twenty—and warning me that my somewhat peculiar productions, no matter how radical or different they might be, could not in the nature of things be much more than technical exercises. I had read of John Milton writing *L'Allegro* and *Il Penseroso* at a most annoyingly early age and could only make the best of it, having been told that the English mind matures anywhere from five to ten years earlier than our minds over here. That was a comfort, for I was compelled to acknowledge, and even to myself, that I could not write *L'Allegro* or *Il Penseroso*, no matter how hard I might try. It was a concession, but I made it.

It was about my seventeenth year when I became violently excited over the structure and music of English blank verse, and in order to find out little more about it I made—of all things possible—a metrical translation of Cicero's first oration against Catiline, which we were reading in school. It began well enough, and with no difficulty:

> O Catiline, how long will you abuse
> Our patience?

That was easy, and invited me to go on. If it lacked something of the vindictive resonance that we feel in the Latin, the fault was not in me but in the English language, for which I was not responsible. So I went on with it until the whole diatribe, which is not short, lay before me in a clean copy of impeccable pentameters (I thought then that they were impeccable) which looked at a glance very much as an equal amount of *Paradise Lost* would have looked if I had copied it on the same quality of paper. It may not have been poetry, and probably wasn't, but many portions of it had music and rhythm and an unmistakable presence of what is nowadays called a punch—for which Cicero may possibly deserve some credit. It was written and rewritten with a prodigality of time that only youth can afford, with an elaborately calculated variation of the cæsura, and with a far more laborious devotion than was ever expended on anything that I was supposed to be studying. When this rather unusual bit of minstrelsy was accomplished, and followed by a similar treatment of long passages from Virgil, I had the profound and perilous satisfaction of knowing a great deal more about the articulation and anatomy of English blank verse than I had known before. A few years later I nearly wore myself out one summer over a metrical translation, made from a literal English version furnished by a schoolmate of mine who is now Professor Smith of Amherst College, of the *Antigone*—which has disappeared mysteriously, and I trust for ever. Nor that it was altogether bad; it was just one of those juvenile experiments that we would rather not have brought in evidence against us. If ever it should come to light, I hope the finder will heed my solemn request that it shall not be published.

It must have been about the year 1889 when I realized finally, and not without a justifiable uncertainty as to how the thing was to be done, that I was doomed, or elected, or sentenced for life to the writing of poetry. There was nothing else that interested me, and I was rational enough to keep the grisly secret to myself. Perhaps I was afraid of being arrested; perhaps I was afraid that my father and mother, the best and kindest of parents, would have had my head examined if they had known what was going on inside it. They knew already that I was unpractical, and indifferent—to say it mildly—to any of the world's reputable pursuits and they knew that I was inordinately addicted to reading the somewhat unusual amount of poetry that was in the house; but they did not know the worst. My father died without suspecting it; my mother did not live to see printed evidence of it—which, while it would have interested her intensely, might still have given her reason to see more darkly than ever, in her affectionate imagination, a prospect that was dark enough even for me whenever I strained my mind's eye for the sight of more than a little of it at a time. For something told me at an early age, long before there was any material reason for worry, that they whose lives are to be chronically hazardous and uncertain should take only short views ahead. Before the family fortune, such as it was, went to smash, I could see it going and could see myself setting out alone on what was inevitably to be a long and foggy voyage. The prospect was interesting, if it was not altogether reassuring.

But I was not much occupied then with the future, which must somehow or other, so far as I was concerned, fulfil itself in its own way. I was chiefly occupied with the composition of short poems and sonnets, which I would read to my old friend and neighbor, Dr. A. T. Schumann, who was himself a prolific writer of sonnets, ballades and rondeaus, and a master of poetic technique. As I shall never know the extent of my indebtedness to his interest and belief in my work, or to my unconscious absorption of his technical enthusiasm, I am glad for this obvious opportunity to acknowledge a debt that I cannot even estimate. Perhaps I was not quite veracious in saying a moment ago that my poetic aspirations and determinations were exclusively a matter of my own knowledge, for the doctor must have known, with his knowledge of humanity and human frailty, the dangerous fate that was before me. In fact, he told me once that I should have to write poetry or starve, and that I might do both—although he did not believe that I should starve, or not exactly. That was encouraging, and I have never forgotten it. If he had cared as much about "the numerous ills inwoven with our frame" as he did about the metrical defects and tonal shortcomings of the major and minor English poets, he would surely have been a most remarkable doctor; as it was, I am sure that he was one of the most remarkable metrical technicians that ever lived, and an invaluable friend to me in those years of apprenticeship when time, as a commodity to be measured and respected, did not exist. There were such things as hours and days and weeks on clocks and calendars, but it made no difference to me how few or many of them went to my getting a few lines to go as I wanted them to go. It was no uncommon performance of mine to write a sonnet in twenty minutes or half an hour, and work over it for twenty days—an expenditure of life for which the doctor could not conscientiously reproach me. One afternoon I found him in his office fairly swelling with triumph and satisfaction, having straightened out a refractory line of his that had been bothering him for two years. All this may have been bad for the practice of medicine, but apparently it was a part of his fate, and of mine.

After two years at Harvard College (1891-1893) where I made

several good friends, I returned to my home in Gardiner, Maine, and worked steadily at my unaccredited profession until 1897, when I went to New York. Sometimes I wondered what my friends and neighbors thought of me, but as it could make no manner of difference to me what they thought, there was nothing for me to do but to go on filing and fitting words until I had words enough to make a book. For three years I sent my wares incessantly to every reputable monthly and weekly periodical in the country—there were not so many in those days as there are now—and invariably got them back, or all but a few that were accepted by some of the less prominent publications or now and then by a newspaper. My collection of rejection slips must have been one of the largest and most comprehensive in literary history, with innumerable duplicates. One sonnet, *The Clerks*, having gone the rounds with many others, was sent finally to The New York *Sun*, and was promptly returned with a piece of white paper on which was written with a blue pencil, "Unavailable. Paul Dana." I am surprised and puzzled to this day that Mr. Dana should have gone to that trouble when he might have had a neat pile of printed slips at his elbow. He may have used them all in returning other sonnets.

Whether or not it was the return of *The Clerks* from The *Sun* that started and set going some new wheels in my emotional machinery is more than I can say at this time. But something set them going, and their persistence assured me at last that there would be no use or sense in any further attempt to make my work known to the public through the periodical press. I was not conscious of analyzing my feelings at the time, but a retrospective consideration of them compels me to suspect myself of being quietly and thoroughly disgusted. I hope it was not so bad as that, but probably it was. At any rate, I made a selection of about forty poems from everything that I had written during the past six or seven years and made a small book of them, reasoning prematurely and wildly that publishers might find something in them that editors had overlooked. But a few experimental attacks in their direction only brought the manuscript back to me with a speed that would be remarkable with even our present aerial facilities. There was something wrong somewhere, and as I was still confident that the poems had nothing worse than a new idiom to condemn them, the fault must be somewhere else. By degrees

I began to realize that those well-typed and harmless looking verses of mine might as well be written, so far as possible attention or interest on the part of editors and publishers was concerned, in the language of the Senegambians.

> I did not think that I should find them there
> When I came back again

was evidently too much: and not only for Mr. Dana, but for the traditional sensibilities of editors in general.

There was nothing left, so far as I could see, but to print the unwelcome little volume at my own expense, and to let it find its way to recognition or to oblivion as it might. With an obstinate confidence that somehow strengthened itself with each new rebuff, I was unable to foresee oblivion for the poems, though I could foresee too surely a long and obscure journey for them before they should have more than a small number of friends. Fortunately for me, a few really responsive and intelligent readers were all that I should expect or require for some years to come, but I wanted those few readers badly, and knew well enough that I was going to have them. So it was with no feeling of humiliation or surrender that I sent the manuscript to the Riverside Press, from which highly respectable establishment I received in due time three hundred copies of an inconspicuous blue-covered little pamphlet, which I had named, rather arbitrarily, from the first and the last poem: *The Torrent and The Night Before*. The entire edition cost me fifty-two dollars, which I am told is appreciably less than one pays today for a single copy. I am naturally a well-wishing person, and not in the least vindictive; yet sometimes I have wished that all surviving editors and publishers who pointed a cold nose at those early poems might find themselves afflicted with a collector's frenzy for the possession of a copy of that first book of mine published in 1896. My constructive imagination would be mean enough to enjoy the sight of them signing cheques for it.

When my three hundred copies arrived (or three hundred and twelve, to be exact) I knew that something important had happened to me. It never occurred to my confident enthusiasm that their arrival, or their existence, might not be important to anybody else, and it was therefore with an untroubled zeal that I began to send them out into the world—

most of them to periodicals for possible critical notice, and to strangers who were known to me only by reputation. Perhaps thirty or forty of them went to friends and acquaintances, but the most of them went, as they were intended to go, unsolicited and unannounced into the un-known. Only a few of them—possibly ten or twelve—failed in drawing from its recipient some sort of response. Considering its unimpressive appearance as a publication and the complete obscurity of its origin, it was received generally with a respect and an enthusiasm that was grati-fying, and was all that I needed to keep me going through the years of obscurity and material uncertainty that were so definitely before me. My incurable belief in what I was doing made me indifferent alike to hos-tility or neglect. There was far more neglect than hostility, as a matter of fact, although now and then a protesting voice would be heard saying something that was not especially complimentary or true. One critic took refuge in paraphrase, merely wishing in print that my poetry might be sent to the bourne from which no poetry returns.

I may say in conclusion, and in reply to several who have asked for information on the subject, that I have no means of knowing how many copies of *The Torrent* are now in existence. Considering the few that have come up for sale, perhaps it may be safe to assume that of the original three hundred, something like half that number may have been lost or destroyed. Thirty-four years may be considered a fairly long life for an obscure pamphlet, and especially for a pamphlet of unorthodox poetry by an unknown writer who could find no publisher for it but himself.

In 1897 most of these poems, along with a number of new ones, were published under the title of *The Children of the Night*.

The Colophon (New York),
Part Four, pp. [71]-[78], November 1930.

HANNIBAL BROWN: AN ALCAIC

Although his wish was never to baffle us
Hannibal Brown was dolichocephalous.

His head reached half way up to heaven.
Hannibal's hat was a number seven.

Buffalo, New York
March 1936

FOR HARRIET MOODY'S COOK BOOK

We should all take off our hats, and we might even consider the possibility of getting down on our knees, in the presence of a good cook. For
without good cooks there would be no good food; and without good food
there would not be many good people; and without a considerable number of good people, with good digestions and dispositions, this world
of ours would be a terrible place. It would be so bad that many of us
would refuse to live in it, and would gladly run the risk of any additional
damnation for the privilege of getting out of it. These words may seem
at first a little violent and exaggerated, but I believe that after a solemn
and open minded consideration of their significance, they will be seen as
only truthful and temperate. If anyone who reads them should be con-
demned to the prospect of eating for the rest of his life the equivalent
of the worst cookery that he has ever encountered, he would begin at
once to be glad for the years that are behind him, and to have glimmer-
ings of a new eschatology.

I have an adequate and familiar name for the few fanatical enthusiasts
who insist that we can make ourselves believe that we have the digestive
machinery of our alleged arboreal ancestors, and that we can make ourselves useful and happy on a diet of raw fruits and vegetables and nuts.
Such a statement may be interesting, and may have a certain economic
appeal, but it has the paralysing disadvantage of being a lie. There is no

royal road or short cut to learning, or to science, or to art, or the achievement of a good dinner. A good dinner cannot be pulled out of the ground, or knocked on the head, or caught with a hook, or shaken from a tree. It is true that we may live and thrive on bread and milk, and it is true that most of us do nothing of the sort. If we were to be sentenced to such a diet, we should have a right to ask for good bread; and good bread does not just happen. Cooks are greater kings, for without cooks the kings would not be very well, and there might be nothing better for them than to make the best of sorrow, and to wait with the rest of us for the end.

The Colophon (New York),
N. S. Vol. III, p. [95], Winter 1938.

[IDEALIST?: AN OCTAVE]

IDEALIST?—Oh yes, or what you will,
I do not wrangle any more with names—
I only want the Truth. Give me the Truth,
And let the system go; give me the Truth,
And I stand satisfied. Fame, glory, gold,—
Take these, and keep them. They were never mine—
I do not ask for them. I only ask
That I, and you, and you, may get the Truth!

Colby Library Quarterly (Waterville, Maine),
Series II, p. 13, February 1947.

138

BROADWAY

By night a gay leviathan
  That fades before the sun,
A monster with a million eyes
  Without the sight of one,
A corybantic thing with claws
  To tear the soul apart,
Breaker of men and avenues,
  It throbs, and has no heart.

By day it has another life
  That feeds on hopes and dreams;
And wears, to cover what it is,
  The mask of what it seems.
But soon its iridescent length
  Will make a fiery show,
To cheer, to dazzle, or to scorch
  The wingless moths below.

And if, at cynic intervals,
  And like a thing in pain,
By chance it implicates itself
  With something not insane,
It will not often, or for long,
  Relinquish what allures
With everything that has the shine
  Of nothing that endures.

American Literature (Durham, North Carolina), Vol. XXII, p. 488, January 1951.

Appendix. Additions and Corrections to Charles Beecher Hogan's *Bibliography of Edwin Arlington Robinson*

Pages 4-5: CAPTAIN CRAIG, 1902. It may be noted that copies of the first edition were in readiness long in advance of publication. The first copies of the limited edition came from the bindery August 9, 1902, and presumably (although there is no corroboration of this) copies of the trade edition were equally premature. Mr. Hogan's copy of the trade edition is inscribed by the author to Miss Swan (*cf.* Hagedorn: *Edwin Arlington Robinson*, 1938, pp. 35-37), and dated by him "27 September 1902," exactly a week before publication.

Page 9: THE TOWN DOWN THE RIVER, 1910. "September 1910" should be deleted from the dates of *reprinting*. This date refers, of course, to that of the printing of the first edition itself.

Page 10: CAPTAIN CRAIG, 1915. See below, pp 143-144, under heading of THE PORCUPINE.

Page 11: THE MAN AGAINST THE SKY, 1916. A few copies have come to light of the May 1916 reprint, in which the mistakes on pp. 57 and 68 have been corrected.

The May 1916 reprint was also issued bound in dark red leather. Bruce Swift's copy of this issue has the misprints corrected.

Page 13: THE THREE TAVERNS, 1920. See below, pp. 143-144, under heading of THE PORCUPINE.

139

Page 14: AVON'S HARVEST, 1921. Two additional examples of binding are now in Mr. Hogan's collection, making a total of five different bindings. The first example has a cloth backstrap of a darker maroon than in any of the other bindings; its weave is the same as that of the third binding as described in his bibliography (circular in form); the word "MACMILLAN" is the same as in the second binding (measuring 2 cms. in height), and it has beneath it four *squares*, not dots. This last is the easiest means of distinguishing this binding, as all of the other four, save the third, which has nothing, have dots.

The second example has a cloth backstrap identical with the second binding as described in the bibliography, save that the word "MACMILLAN" measures 1 cm. in height. (The variations in the binding of AVON'S HARVEST occur only as regards the backstrap; the covers in all five variants are the same.)

The Macmillan Company reports that this book never had more than one printing, but that over a period of ten years the sheets were bound up, as needed, on five different occasions. From the binder's records it is not possible to determine the exact order, inasmuch as the cloth and the dies for the stamping of the publisher's name were used indiscriminately at the time of each binding. (See below, pp. 143-144, under heading of THE PORCUPINE.) From inscriptions by the author in various copies and from other evidence, however, the priority of the first two bindings can definitely be established. In the summary given below the dates in italics are those of binding, as furnished by the Macmillan Company.

AVON'S HARVEST (published March 29, 1921)

First binding *March 1921*
> Cross-grain weave, small MACMILLAN, four dots.
> (Mr. Hogan's copy inscribed "April 1921.")

Second binding *May 1921*
> Pebbled weave, small MACMILLAN, four dots.
> (Mr. Hogan's copy inscribed "1921.")

Third (?) binding *June 1927:* 100 copies.
> Circular weave, small MACMILLAN, no dots.

Fourth (?) binding *May 1928*
    Pebbled weave, large MACMILLAN, four dots.
    (This is the binding described in the bibliography as the second.)
Fifth binding *June 1931*
    Circular weave, large MACMILLAN, four squares.
    (Mr. Hogan's copy purchased from Macmillan stock in 1937.)

Pages 16-17: COLLECTED POEMS, 1921. In the description of the title-page of the book and of the list of subscribers, the comma following the word *"SHOP"* should be roman and not italic. It may also be pointed out that a few sets of this book were issued without the labels already attached to the spine, but instead tipped in to the books themselves, to be pasted on by the individual purchaser.

Page 21: THE MAN WHO DIED TWICE, 1924. This English edition consisted of 250 copies only. Mr. Hogan has a third (?) binding, identical with the first save that the cloth is a very dark blue.

Page 22: DIONYSUS IN DOUBT, 1925. In all copies there is the following misprint: page 27, line 16 the word "them" instead of "than." This mistake has never been corrected in print; in Mr. Hogan's copy it is corrected in Robinson's hand.

Page 31: THREE POEMS, 1928. The history of the printing of this pamphlet remains obscure. Exactly how many copies were originally prepared and how many destroyed, cannot with any certainty be determined. Robinson himself (who, although genuinely interested in the bibliography of his own books, was almost invariably misinformed about them), stated that 25 copies were printed and 12 destroyed. (See H. B. Collamore: *Edwin Arlington Robinson*, 1936, p. 43.) That would leave 13 copies in existence. Since the compilation of the bibliography (which located all 12(?) known copies) at least one other has definitely come to light, and was in the possession of Mr. Parkman D. Howe, of Providence. The discovery of this copy would seem to substantiate Robinson's own statement that 13 had survived destruction.

But it is most unlikely that 25 copies were originally printed. The authority for stating in the bibliography that 17 were prepared and 5 destroyed was Mr. Bradley Fisk, who, with Mr. Lucius Beebe and Mr. J. A. DeLacey, concocted the scheme of getting these three poems into print. Mr. DeLacey's recollection, however, in a letter dated November 1940, is that there were 18 copies. Both Mr. Fisk and Mr. DeLacey are agreed that 5 copies were burned, "with great ceremony." Mr. DeLacey's figure of 13 surviving copies consequently agrees with Robinson's.

The evidence therefore points so strongly to the existence of 13 copies, 9 of which are still in circulation, that there is no reason why this figure should not be accepted.

Page 33: FORTUNATUS, 1928. The rules on the title-page are in brown, not red.

Page 34: SONNETS 1889-1927, 1928. A variant issue of the first edition has been discovered since 1936. It may be distinguished from the other issues by the date "October 1928" on the verso of the title-page, by its six (not five) preliminary leaves, and by its watermarked paper. The specifications of the Macmillan Company for these issues — all of which were printings of the same edition — are as follows:

> 1st issue: dated "October 1928," 5 preliminary leaves, no watermark.
>
> 2nd issue: dated "October 1928," 6 preliminary leaves, watermark.
>
> 3rd issue: dated "November 1928," 6 preliminary leaves, no watermark.

Page 37: COLLECTED POEMS, 1929. The statement that the India paper and the dark green leather issues of this volume are, save for the number of dots on the spine, identical with the maroon cloth issue is incorrect. In the issue on India paper the frontispiece is protected by tissue-paper, and the issue bound in leather has the top edge gilt.

Page 48: HANNIBAL BROWN, 1936. The statement that this pamphlet is printed throughout on vellum is inaccurate. Mr. Hogan followed the notice of limitation on page 5, which states that all copies are on vellum, and did not notice that his copy was printed on a heavy, deckle-edged, watermarked *paper*. What is true of his copy is true of all copies. Mr. Schmitt, the sponsor of the pamphlet, says that it was his original intention to use vellum, but at the very last moment this plan was abandoned, and the entire edition of 25 copies was printed on paper.

Page 49: VAN ZORN, 1914. See below, under heading of THE PORCU-
PINE.

VAN ZORN has been reissued by AMS Press, New York, 1970.

Page 49: THE PORCUPINE, 1915. It has at last been definitely established that copies of this book exist without the erratum slip facing page 3. When such copies appear it is a simple matter to determine whether or not the slip was never put in at all or was subsequently torn out, because in the latter case experiments have proved it impossible to remove the slip without leaving traces of the glue, and because the pressure of the slip against pages 2 and 3 has almost invariably left an indentation on those pages.

On application to the publishers Mr. Hogan was told that the manufacturing records for 1915 are no longer in existence, and that therefore it is not possible to say exactly when the erratum slip was printed and inserted into the book. But it is nevertheless certain that a few early examples (review copies, etc.) were issued without the slip. For such examples, however, it would be inadmissible to claim priority. There is no adequate evidence as to whether the first copies appeared with or without the erratum slip.

To elaborate the remarks made above under the heading of AVON'S HARVEST, as regards the "MACMILLAN" dies used on the spines of several of Robinson's books, these dies are of various shapes and sizes, and were used indiscriminately. Because of this fact, it is an arguable point as to whether or not the presence of different "MACMILLAN" dies on bindings that otherwise show no variations constitute truly different bindings. A difference remains, however, a difference, and listed below are the dies as they appear on Mr. Hogan's copies of VAN ZORN, CAPTAIN CRAIG

(1915), THE PORCUPINE, THE THREE TAVERNS, and AVON'S
HARVEST (after which these dies were no longer used on any of
Robinson's books). These differences occur only in the shape of
the letter "M," the stem of which is either straight or splayed.

VAN ZORN	THE THREE TAVERNS
1st—splayed	1st—straight
2nd—straight	2nd—splayed
3rd—straight	3rd—splayed
CAPTAIN CRAIG (1915)	AVON'S HARVEST
1st—splayed	1st—straight
2nd—splayed	2nd—straight
3rd—straight	3rd—straight
THE PORCUPINE	4th—straight
1st—splayed	5th—splayed
2nd—straight	

Page 50: THE PETERBOROUGH IDEA, 1917. The description of this item
is incorrect. What appears here is the third, not the first, edition
of the pamphlet. The mistake may be laid to two facts. First, THE
PETERBOROUGH IDEA was first described bibliographically by the
late Major Whitall, a close personal friend of Robinson. Mr. Hogan
has Major Whitall's own copy, presented to him (although not
autographed) by the author. Second, in Mr. H. B. Collamore's collection there is a copy, identical with Mr. Hogan's, on which Robinson has written, "First Printing."

Major Whitall was an enthusiastic, but highly unscientific pio-
neer in this field, and Robinson himself was, although equally enthusiastic, usually a little haphazard.

The matter has finally been cleared up beyond any possibility of
doubt, through the personal recollections of Mrs. Edward Mac-
Dowell and through the researches of Mr. L. W. Payne, the results
of which he has published in The University of Texas Studies in
English, July 8, 1939, pp. 219-231. Mr. Payne gives such careful
bibliographical details regarding THE PETERBOROUGH IDEA that
it is wholly unnecessary to repeat them here. In brief, however, the
various editions of the pamphlet may be distinguished as follows:

1st—unillustrated, imprint on back cover: COSMUS & WASH-BURN / 605 FIFTH AVENUE, N. Y. /.

2nd—unillustrated, no imprint.

3rd—illustrated.

4th—unillustrated, imprint on back cover: TRANSCRIPT PRINTING COMPANY / PETERBOROUGH, N. H. /.

The above, all of which are undated, were issued in white paper wrappers. Subsequent editions, at least all that have been seen, are printed in a small, inexpensive format, generally on cream-colored paper.

Page 52: In addition to the poems by Robinson set to music, as listed on this page and on page 195, there are also the following: *The House on the Hill*, music by Aaron Copland, Boston: E. C. Schirmer Music Co., 1926; *The Dark Hills*, music by Louise Souther, Boston: Charles W. Homeyer & Co., Inc., 1937; *The Song of Jael* (selected and arranged from *Sisera*), music by Mabel Daniels, New York: J. Fischer & Bro., 1937; *Richard Cory*, music by Charles Naginski, New York: G. Schirmer, Inc., 1940.

Page 62: THE PILGRIM SPIRIT, 1921. The bibliography of this item is exceedingly complicated, and the description of it is by no means complete, and, in a few particulars, it is inaccurate. The book exists in five *states*, all of which are issues of one edition, and not separate editions. The one described in the bibliography is the third issue, which appears in two bindings: paper and cloth.

The first issue of the book, of which there is but *one* state, was published July 11, 1921, in a printing of 10,953 (not 11,000) copies, bound in *paper wrapper*. This issue is filled with misprints, a list of which is given below.

The second issue, of which there are *two* states, appeared first on August 6, 1921, in a printing of 1,498 copies, bound in *cloth*, and with an erratum slip on page 74. It appeared in its second state on August 31, 1921, in a printing of 1,000 copies, bound in *paper*, also with the erratum slip on page 74. In both states of this issue the misprints of the first issue are retained.

The third issue (the one described in the bibliography), of which there are also *two* states, appeared first on August 22, 1921, in a printing of 5,000 copies, bound in *paper*, without the erratum slip, and with the misprints corrected. It appeared in its second state on September 30, 1921, in a printing of 2,500 copies, bound in *cloth*, identical otherwise (save for the insertion of illustrations) with the first state of this issue. The grand total of copies is 20,951.

Confusing as all this is, there is one fact still more confusing. The first issue has many misprints; the second issue retains these misprints, but contains one erratum slip. The third issue has the misprints corrected and, of course, contains no erratum slip, but it has a new misprint of its own that does not appear in the first two issues, namely, "THP" for "THE" in the running-title on page 55. This would be easily explained if the third issue were in fact not an issue, but another *edition*, entirely reset in order to correct the misprints. But a careful examination of a large number of copies of THE PILGRIM SPIRIT clearly shows that the book was never reset at all, and that the misprints were corrected merely from the already existing plates. The proof of this statement will be seen in the existence of numerous examples of broken type which appear regularly in *all five issues*, from approximately the first page of the book to the last. The most obvious is on the very page (55) that contains the misprinted running-title: line 19, the "s" in "strictly." Other examples are: page 23, line 8—the "t" in "seventeen"; page 75 (the page following that bearing the erratum slip of the second issue), line 2—the "h" in "hand"; page 86, line 6—the "A" in "Allerton"; page 113, line 14—the "l" in "Truculently." Further proof may be seen in innumerable examples throughout the whole text of the letter "n," which is too heavily inked.

It will be observed from the list given below that in the first two issues of THE PILGRIM SPIRIT there is a misprint in line 2 of page 55: "fredom," which was corrected to "freedom" in the third issue. For a reason difficult to explain, not only was line 2 reset in making this correction, but also, albeit needlessly, line 1 and the running-title. The evidence lies in line 1, which consists of the speech-prefix "CLIFTON." In the first two issues the initial letter of this word appears half-way below the "L" and the "G" of "PILGRIM" in the running-title. In the third issue, however, the word has been moved about 2 cms. to the left, so that its initial letter appears half-way below the "I" and the "L" of "PILGRIM." The rest of the page was left untouched, but the above evidence seems to explain conclusively the new misprint that this page carries in the third issue.

Appended herewith is a list of findings (it is doubtless incomplete) of misprints in the first and second issues, and of certain misprints, chiefly of punctuation, that were never corrected in any of the issues.

		1st and 2nd Issues	*3rd Issue*
Page	i, 5	(blank)	WILLIAM CARROLL HILL, *Secretary*
Page	5, 19	England	England,
Page	20, 15	*handsake*	*handshake*
Page	34, 10	*arm sof*	*arms of*
Page	35, 2	but not your!	but not yours!
Page	55, 2	fredom	freedom
Page	56, 3	be kept seized	be seized
Page	58, 6	our faces	our face
Page	59, 23	*seawood*)	*seaward*)
Page	61, 26	*There,*	*These,*
Page	66, 11	touch	torch
Page	66, note	The description and the directions, with music, for this dance were furnished. . .	The music for this dance was furnished. . .
Page	70, 22	Master BREWER	Master BREWSTER
Page	74, 8	ROBINSON, BREWSTER, BRADFORD	ROBINSON, BRADFORD
Page	76, 18	knoweldge	knowledge
Page	78, 15	ROCKS	ROCK
Page	78, 16	*The . . . speaks.*	(*The. . . speaks.*)
Page	78, 23	way,	way
Page	85, 5	hath done	hath been

148

Page 96, 16	*penetrate*	*penetrating*
Page 98, 13	*gesticulatnig*	*gesticulating*
Page 105, 14	Company	Compact
Page 124, 10	Yes.	Yea.
Page 134, 12	in off-shore	an off-shore
Page 135, 3	(Your hope	Your hope
Page 135, 6	live.)	live.
Page 135, 11	ship at all	ship of all
Page 135, 20	Coming in	Come in

All Issues

Page 5, 16	Accomack.	(for)	Accomack,
Page 32, 24	Puritans	"	Puritan's
Page 39, 22	*(turing*	"	*(turning*
Page 44, 23	*himelf*	"	*himself*
Page 54, 25	*and*	"	and
Page 58, 13	*childern*	"	*children*
Page 62, 5	leaders.)	"	*leaders.)*
Page 66, 20	*lights.*	"	*lights.)*
Page 67, 15	STANDISH.	"	STANDISH,
Page 72, 28	ROBINSON.	"	ROBINSON.)
Page 73, 19	*close in.*	"	*close in.)*
Page 78, 19	leaders.	"	leaders,
Page 79, 7	heritage.	"	heritage,
Page 83, 16	*light*	"	*lights*
Page 83, 21	Britain	"	Britain,
Page 84, 1	one of	"	of one
Page 84, 14	*goes on*:	"	*goes on*:)
Page 86, 22	servant..	"	servant.
Page 86, 24	*is absorbed*	"	*is so absorbed*
Page 87, 5	FULLER	"	FULLER.
Page 87, 11	servants.)	"	servants. (HOWLAND,
	HOWLAND	"	
Page 120, 27	*round. "Look*	"	*round, "Look*
Page 120, 28	*firebrand.)*	"	*firebrand.*
Page 121, 19	*men.)*	"	*men.*
Page 124, 20	forth	"	forth,

Page 125, 11	BRADFORD.	"	BRADFORD.)
Page 130, 9	is silent.)	"	*is silent.*)
Page 133, 22	*Adventures*	"	*Adventurers*

Page 64: A WREATH FOR EDWIN MARKHAM, 1922. Robinson's quatrain on page 20 of this book was first reprinted in *New Poems: Eighty Songs at 80*, by Edwin Markham, New York: Doubleday, Doran & Company, Inc., 1932, p. ix.

Page 65: ANTHOLOGY OF MAGAZINE VERSE FOR 1923, 1923. There was also a limited edition of 245 copies, identical with the edition described on pp. 65-66 of the *Bibliography*, save that on page [iv] is a notice of limitation of edition, with autograph number, and, beneath, editor's autograph signature; on page [vi] the date of publication is omitted; following page 188 (second pagination) are two blank leaves; the paper is white, not cream as in the regular edition, and is watermarked; the book is bound in olive-drab paper-covered boards, with brown buckram backstrap and corners; the top edge is gilt; and the leaves measure 24.1 by 16.8 cms. Mr. Briathwaite said that this was the only one of his Anthologies to be issued in both a regular and a limited and signed edition.

The printers of this issue of the *Anthology* said that the figure of 3375 (as given on page 66 of the *Bibliography*) constitutes the total number printed. The regular edition of the 1923 *Anthology* consequently consisted of 3130 copies.

Page 71: MODERN AMERICAN POETRY, 1936. *Too Much Coffee* has been reprinted in *From Another World*, by Louis Untermeyer, New York: Harcourt, Brace and Company, 1939, p. 227.

Page 74: HARVARD, CLASS OF 1895, SIXTH REPORT, 1920. The "1895" on the spine is in capitals, not lower case.

Page 77: HARVARD, CLASS OF 1895, SEVENTH REPORT, 1925. The "1895" on the spine is in capitals, not lower case.

Page 82: THE COLOPHON—PART FOUR, 1930. *The First Seven Years* has been reprinted in *Breaking into Print*, edited by Elmer Adler, New York: Simon and Schuster, 1937, pp. 163-170.

Page 85: ON THE MEANING OF LIFE, 1932. The letter to Dr. Durant has been reprinted in *Selected Letters of Edwin Arlington Robinson*, 1940, pp. 163-165.

Page 87: A BIBLIOGRAPHY OF THE WORKS OF ROBINSON JEFFERS, 1933. There is also a limited edition of 15 copies, 10 for sale and 5 for presentation. It is identical with the edition described on pages 87-88, save that the preface and "Remembered Verses" are signed in autograph by their respective authors; an original holograph Jeffers manuscript is inserted in a flap on the inside of the back cover; and the book is bound in rose-green marbled boards, with gold line on the inside edges of both covers, and a black leather backstrap.

Page 90: LETTERS TO HARRIET, 1935. The letters dated July 29, 1910; October 17, 1910; and December 10, 1915 have been reprinted in *Selected Letters of Edwin Arlington Robinson*, 1940, pp. 67-68, 69 and 90-91 respectively.

Page 94: E. A. R., 1936. The letter dated June 1929 has been reprinted in *Selected Letters of Edwin Arlington Robinson*, 1940, p. 159.

Page 107: THE NEW TENANTS, 1919. A copy of *The Lyric* for July–August 1919 is now in Mr. Hogan's collection. The poem appears on p. [9] of that issue. It is reprinted verbatim in *The Three Taverns*, 1920, p.83.

Page 111: AFTER THE WAR, 1924. This poem was published in Volume I, Number 1 of *The Saturday Review of Literature*. In addition to the regular issue of the magazine, there was also a limited issue of 279 copies, autographed by the editors, and printed on handmade paper.

Page 114: A NEW ENGLAND POET, 1918. This article was reprinted as a broadside, at the instance of Dr. Schumann's widow, presumably almost immediately after its appearance in the *Boston Evening Transcript* of March 30, 1918. It resembles in every particular of type and set-up the original article, and was apparently prepared in the printing-office of the *Transcript* itself as an off-set. There is no definite proof of this: the editor of the *Transcript* said that no records of this having been done are in existence.

The collation is as follows: Boston Transcript (in black letter) / 324 WASHINGTON STREET, BOSTON, MASS. / (double ornamental rule) / SATURDAY, MARCH 30, 1918 / (double ornamental rule) / *A NEW ENGLAND POET* / (rule) / Alanson Tucker Schumann's Unostenta- / tious Career / (rule) / (text) / EDWIN ARLINGTON ROBINSON / (rule) /. It is printed on smooth wove paper, the verso blank, measuring 42.3 by 9.6 cms.

Page 115: [EXCERPT FROM LETTER TO ALBERT O. BASSUK, 1932]. This was first reprinted in *The New York Times*, June 20, 1932, p. 17.

Page 116: [FIVE LETTERS TO DANIEL GREGORY MASON, 1936]. These letters have been reprinted as follows: June 19, 1899, pp. 860-861, in *Selected Letters of Edwin Arlington Robinson*, 1940, pp. 17-18; August 27, 1899, p. 861, in *ibid.*, pp. 19-20; October 30, 1899, p. 862, in part in Mr. Mason's *Music in My Time*, 1938, p. 87, and in the *Letters*, p. 25; October 25, 1900, pp. 862-863, in part in *Philosophy in the Poetry of Edwin Arlington Robinson*, by Estelle Kaplan, 1940, pp. 13-14; July 22, 1908, pp. 863-864, in the *Letters*, pp. 63-64.

Index

154

166